C00 2180394:?

EDINBURGH CITY LI

D1578571

FA3

HQ

30

Intimate Relations

living and loving in later life

Dr Sarah Brewer

BOOKS

© 2004 Sarah Brewer

Published by Age Concern England
1268 London Road
London SW16 4ER

First published 2004

Editor Richenda Milton-Thompson
Production Vinnette Marshall
Design and typesetting GreenGate Publishing Services
Printed and bound in Great Britain by Bell & Bain Ltd, Glasgow

A catalogue record for this book is available from the British Library

ISBN 0-86242-384-8

All rights reserved; no part of this work may be reproduced in any form, by mimeograph or any other means, without permission in writing from the publisher.

Whilst the advice and information contained in *Intimate Relations: living and loving in later life* is believed to be true and accurate at the time of going to press, neither Age Concern England nor the author can accept any legal responsibility or liability for any errors or omissions that may be made. While every effort has been made to check the accuracy of material contained in this publication, neither Age Concern England nor the author can accept responsibility for the results of any action taken by readers as a result of reading this book. Please note that while the products mentioned in this book are known to Age Concern, inclusion here does not constitute a recommendation by Age Concern for any particular product, agency, service or publication.

Contents

About the author

Dr Sarah Brewer graduated from Cambridge University as a doctor in 1983. She was a full-time GP for five years and now works in nutritional medicine and sexual health. She writes widely on all aspects of health, including complementary medicine and has written 40 popular self-help books.

Acknowledgements

With thanks to my long-suffering, understanding and unusually loving husband, Richard. I don't deserve him!

Introduction

We live in an ageing society with more and more people surviving into their 70s, 80s, 90s and beyond. Due to medical advances, most older people are just as fit and active as when they were younger, remaining fully independent in many – if not all – aspects of life. It there fore comes as a shock to realise just how much the ageing process can gradually creep up on you. It is difficult to believe just how quickly time has passed. The passage of time brings with it inevitable changes in your body – no matter how hard you – or your cosmetic surgeon – work to hold them at bay. Skin and muscles that were once toned become slack, and the face in the mirror starts to show the signs of wisdom and experience. It doesn't matter! You will still feel just the same inside as when you were in the peak of youth. Your ability to feel love, and to share erotic experiences, is still there, just as it always was.

A rewarding sex life is an important part of well-being and a loving relationship – at all stages of adult life. The information in this book is applicable to everyone, whatever their age, health or sexual orientation. When you enjoy regular sexual intimacy with your partner, all aspects of life tend to take on a rosier hue.

Sex and health

Sex is often a taboo subject in later life, but physical intimacy does not fizzle out and disappear once people reach a certain age – despite what the younger generation may believe. A survey of over 1300 older people by the National Council on Aging in the United States found that nearly 60 per cent of men and women over the age of 60 still enjoyed a fully active sex life. This shouldn't be surprising given the importance of intimacy in relationships between couples of all ages.

The benefits of regular sex have been suggested through the ages. In ancient China, the flow of sexual energy around the body was believed to form the basis of physical, emotional and spiritual well being, and channelling sexual energy was considered the key to immortality. In fact, aphrodisiacs and erotic arts were used not to simply increase the pleasure of sex, but as a way to improve general health and longevity. In Chinese medicine, sexual energy is viewed as a manifestation of constitutional essence which, if excessively depleted, is believed to lead to premature ageing and recurrent ill health.

Why regular sex is beneficial for males

Researchers have also confirmed the many beneficial effects of regular sexual activity. A study involving nearly 1000 men in Caerphilly in Wales found that the risk of death at any age in men with a high orgasmic frequency (twice a week or more) was half that of men with a low orgasmic frequency (less than one a month). The authors concluded that sexual activity seems to have a protective effect on men's health. This may be linked with the effects of the master sex hormone, known as DHEA (dehydroepiandrosterone), which is made in the adrenal glands. Its main function is to act as a building block for producing other steroid hormones including oestrogen, progesterone and testosterone. DHEA levels rise just before orgasm and ejaculation to three to five times higher than normal, which some claim is one of the reasons that regular sex can prolong your life.

Researchers have also found that male hair growth seems to increase when sex is anticipated, probably as a result of increased testosterone activity. Testosterone levels have been found to increase during and after sex which may provide some protection against male osteoporosis and coronary heart disease, as well as improving muscle bulk and maintaining the size of the penis and testicles in later life. Regular sex also helps to relieve congestion of the male prostate gland, and may reduce the risk of prostatitis (inflammation of the gland) too.

Another beneficial effect of sex is that it is an excellent reliever of stress, mild aches and pains. Testosterone has a painkilling action by damping down inflammation, especially in joints. Research suggests that some arthritis sufferers have less pain for up to six hours after sex.

Why regular sex is beneficial for females

Regular sexual activity also seems to be important for a women's physiology, even in later life after the menopause. Regular sex can increase blood oestrogen levels, helping to protect against coronary heart disease and osteoporosis. Sexual abstinence on the other hand has been found to lower oestrogen levels and may be linked with increased menopausal problems. Research in the US involving both young, undergraduate women and older women approaching the menopause, found those who had sex regularly every week (except during menstruation) had oestrogen levels around twice as high as those who were less sexually active, and that menopausal women having regular sex had fewer hot flushes and tended to age more slowly than those who did not have sex at least once a week.

Sexual activity also helps to keep the female pelvic floor muscles toned, helping to reduce the risk of urinary leakage due to stress incontinence or prolapse, and can make sex more enjoyable for both partners.

Why regular sex is beneficial for couples

In both men and women, levels of the hormone oxytocin peak during orgasm. This has a tranquillising effect, helping to provide a good night's sleep. This effect is greater in males than females. Oxytocin is also the hormone that helps to bind a couple together in love, and a regular sex life will continue to cement your relationship no matter how long you have been together.

When you are enjoying a healthy sex life, your general well-being and quality of life are enhanced. It is not the be-all and end-all of a relationship however. If, as a couple, you are happy with a low level of sexual interaction, this should not be regarded as a problem. Long-lasting marriages are built on friendship, love, laughter, humour and shared experiences as much as on a normal sex drive. But if lack of sex is causing problems, it is important to seek help from your doctor or a psychosexual counsellor.

Safe sex

Although an important theme of this book is that sex is beneficial and contributes to happiness and well-being, a note of caution must be sounded. It is not only young people, gay people and drug users who are at risk of sexually transmitted diseases, so 'safe sex' should be practised in any new or temporary relationship. More advice on this important topic is given in Chapter 8.

Sexual problems

As you get older, there may be fewer people that you care about compared to when you were younger, and they will therefore become increasingly important to you. Those who are in a long term relationship will have adapted to the needs and habits of their partner and may well feel they fit each other like a comfortable pair of gloves – fitting snugly, yet giving in all the right places.

A rewarding sex life is an important part of well-being and of a loving relationship, yet many couples come face to face with sexual problems in later life. Often, these problems are accepted with resignation, yet loss of sexuality should not be viewed as an inevitable part of the ageing process. It is not, even though frequency of sexual activity will vary from couple to couple at this time of life.

In the UK, a survey involving a random selection of 182 women aged between 48 and 58, found that 18 per cent of them were sexually active several times a week, 48 per cent once a week, 27 per cent less than once a week while only 7 per cent were not sexually active at all. In the US, research carried out by the National Council on Aging suggested that, although nearly 60 per cent of men and women over the age of 60 were still fully sexually active, the majority reported having sex less often than when they were younger. Around 40 per cent felt they would like to have sex more often than they actually did. More than one in three men in their 60s and half of men in their 70s also admitted they had been unable to consistently obtain and maintain an erection during the previous 6 months, while one in three women found that lack of lubrication could be a problem. This raises an important point because, although male sexual problems such as impotence receive most media coverage, females can also encounter sexual problems in later life. In the UK, an anonymous survey of female patients registered with four GP surgeries found that 41 per cent admitted to having a current sexual problem. Of these, the most common types of female sexual dysfunction were vaginal dryness (28 per cent), difficulty obtaining orgasm (27 per cent), painful intercourse (18 per cent), inhibited enjoyment (18 per cent) and problems with arousal (17 per cent). A similar survey in the US found that 32 per cent of women reported low or no sexual desire. This contributed to other sexual difficulties including vaginal dryness (21 per cent) and painful sexual intercourse (16 per cent). Overall, almost 1 in 4 women (23 per cent) in this study no longer found sex pleasurable.

Although sexual problems can become more frequent as you get older, this does not mean they should be tolerated. The majority of sexual problems can usually be overcome quite easily with one of the many medical treatments now available. Even if you have health problems such as arthritis, heart disease, stroke or even cancer, these need not get in the way of a fulfilling relationship. You do not need to swing from the chandeliers, adopt contortionist positions, or even be particularly physically active or mobile, in order to share a fulfilling and enjoyable love life with your partner. Even if penetrative sex tends to become less frequent, qualities such as love, affection and reciprocal tenderness still remain very important.

Many couples actually enjoy sex more as they get older, as they have more time to spend on this rewarding and fulfilling part of their life. The demands of children, jobs and paying the mortgage may be behind them, so they have more time for relaxation and fun. In fact, couples who are comfortable with each other don't even have to indulge in penetrative sex. Touching, caressing and stroking can bring just as much pleasure when there is no pressure to perform.

It is very important that you are both able to feel comfortable with the level of sexual activity you choose. Any frequency of lovemaking is normal so long as both you and your partner are happy. Many couples share love, affection and a meaningful emotional relationship without a physically active sex life. Frequently however, particularly where sex has virtually petered out, one of the partners will be unhappy about the lack of a physical relationship while the other is unhappy about the sexual demands being placed on them. In one survey, for example, over a third of menopausal women felt that men wanted sex more often than they did themselves and that this was often a problem.

If lack of sex is causing problems, do seek advice from your doctor. While it is best to seek professional advice where sexual problems are long-standing, it is possible to do some of the exercises suggested by psychosexual therapists on your own at home. If these do not help within a few weeks, it is important to seek professional advice.

1 Living in Later Life

Many people find middle-age and later life has crept up on them and suddenly realise they have 'let themselves go' and become unfit or overweight. Lack of stamina and feeling unattractive both have a significant dampening effect on sexuality. But the good news is that it is possible to reverse these trends, lose excess weight and increase your level of fitness – whatever your age. As a bonus, most people who manage to shed an excess 10lb (4.5kg) also look and feel as if they have shed ten years, boosting their physical, emotional and sexual energy levels. Caring about your body and well-being is essential for improved vitality and self-esteem. Unless you feel confident about your body and fitness level, it will be difficult to relax and enjoy sex to the full.

Maintaining a healthy weight

Everyone feels better about themselves sexually if they feel physically as well as spiritually attractive. To feel physically attractive, you need to be happy about your weight and accept yourself as you are whether you are underweight, overweight, obese or have a normal weight for your height. It is quite possible to enjoy a fulfilling and happy sex life whatever your size. For optimum stamina, mobility and health, however, it is wise to aim to get into the healthy weight range for your height.

Are you in the healthy weight range for your height?

The healthy weight for your height can be worked out using a complicated equation known as the body mass index (BMI). This is assessed by dividing your weight (in kilograms) by the square of your height (in metres).

$$BMI = \frac{Weight\ (kg)}{Height \times Height\ (m^2)}$$

So, for example, someone with a weight of 70kg and a height of 1.7m has a BMI of 70 ÷ (1.7 × 1.7) = 24.22kg/m^2.

The calculation produces a number that can be interpreted by the table below.

BMI	Weight band
< 20	Underweight
20–25	Healthy
25–30	Overweight
30–40	Obese
> 40	Morbidly obese

A BMI of 20–25 is in the healthy weight range as it is not linked with an increased risk of premature mortality. To avoid you having to do the calculation, the table on page 3 shows the healthy weight band for your height based on a BMI of 20 to 25.

If your BMI is in the overweight range (25–30), you should try to lose a few pounds to bring you back into the healthy weight range for your height. Those who are overweight are one and a half times more likely to have a heart attack than someone who maintains a healthy weight. They will also find physical exertion – including sexual activity – more arduous. Where excess weight is stored is also important. If you are overweight and also store fat round your middle (apple shaped), you are twice as likely to develop coronary heart disease – especially if this runs in your family. Getting down to the healthy weight range for your height can reduce your risk of a heart attack by as much as 35–55 per cent.

Height		Weight	
Metres	Feet	Kilogrammes	Stones
1.47	4'10"	43–54	6st 11lb–8st 7lb
1.50	4'11"	45–56	7st 1lb–8st 11lb
1.52	5ft	46–58	7st 3lb–9st 2lb
1.55	5'1"	48–60	7st 8lb–9st 7lb
1.57	5'2"	49–62	7st 10lb–9st 11lb
1.60	5'3"	51–64	8st–10st 1lb
1.63	5'4"	53–66	8st 5lb–10st 6lb
1.65	5'5"	54–68	8st 7lb–10st 10lb
1.68	5'6"	56–70	8st 12lb–11st
1.70	5'7"	58–72	9st 1lb–11st 4lb
1.73	5'8"	60–75	9st 6lb–11st 10lb
1.75	5'9"	61–76	9st 9lb–12st
1.78	5'10"	63–79	9st 13lb–12st 6lb
1.80	5'11"	65–81	10st 3lb–12st 9lb
1.83	6ft	67–83	10st 7lb–13st 1lb
1.85	6'1"	69–85	10st 11lb–13st 5lb
1.88	6'2"	71–88	11st 2lb–13st 12lb
1.90	6'3"	72–90	11st 5lb–14st 2lb
1.93	6'4"	75–93	11st 10lb–14st 8lb

Are you an apple or a pear?

Work out your waist/hip ratio by measuring your waist and hips in centimetres, then divide the figures as follows:

$$\frac{waist}{hip} = ratio$$

So, if you have a waist measurement of 99cm and hip of 109cm, your waist/hip ratio is 99/109 = 0.9.

■ If you are female, is your waist/hip ratio less than 0.85?
■ If you are male, is your waist/hip ratio less than 0.95?

If not, then you are apple shaped. This can interfere with your love life by making popular positions such as the missionary position (ie, lying down, face to face, with the man on top of the woman) less easy to accomplish. People who are apple-shaped also have a higher risk of hardening and furring up of the arteries, high cholesterol levels, high blood pressure, coronary heart disease, stroke and diabetes than those who are pear-shaped. The reason is not fully understood, but is probably linked with the way your body handles dietary fats. Lack of exercise and drinking excessive amounts of alcohol also seem to encourage fat gain around the waist. People who are under stress and also apple shaped therefore need to take urgent steps to increase their level of activity. Luckily, people who are apple-shaped seem to lose weight more easily than those who are pear-shaped. This is because abdominal fat is mobilised and broken down more easily than fat stored elsewhere.

If you are overweight and also apple shaped, you have a high risk of developing coronary heart disease – especially if this runs in your family.

In fact, waist size alone may be a good indicator of health – or lack of it. New research suggests that men with a waist circumference larger than 102cm and women with a waist circumference larger than 88cm are more likely to have shortness of breath, high blood pressure, high cho- lesterol levels and diabetes than those with slimmer waistlines. Slight waist reductions (of just 5–10cm) significantly reduce the risk of having a heart attack.

Exercise

As well as helping to reduce an apple shape and lose weight, exercise increases your strength (by building up muscle bulk), your stamina (by increasing muscle energy stores) and your suppleness (by improving the range of movement of joints and making ligaments and tendons more flexible).

Like other forms of exercise, sex can improve your general level of fit- ness as it can increase your pulse rate to an average of 114 beats per minute (and sometimes to as high as 140–150 beats per minute) and encourage you to breathe more deeply. These changes help to boost your metabolic rate, are virtually identical to those that occur during intense exercise and can bring similar health benefits. Sex – like any other form of vigorous physical exercise – increases blood oxygen levels, strengthens muscle tone and helps to keep you mentally alert. Your resting pulse rate will reduce as your heart and circulatory system become more efficient.

NB If you have a serious heart condition, check with your doctor that you are fit enough for sex – and take things gently.

There are many things you can do to improve your general and sexual health in later life. You may already be aware of the need to lose some excess weight, tone up your abdominal muscles or cut back on drinking or smoking. You also need to ensure an adequate supply of vitamins and minerals, through careful attention to your diet.

Benefits of exercise

During brisk exercise, muscle cells can increase their level of metabolic activity and the amount of heat they generate to over 20 times that produced during rest. This in turn increases your body's overall metabolic rate as much as tenfold. As a result, you burn more fuel (especially fat) to produce more energy – an excellent way to lose any excess flab and to maintain a healthy weight.

If you are unfit, starting an exercise programme may leave you feeling temporarily fatigued, but this will soon pass and you will feel more energised as your fitness level improves. This is because muscles start to store more energy in the form of a starchy compound, glycogen, so you can exercise longer without tiring. Someone who takes very little exercise, for example, may only have 1g of glycogen per 100g of muscle, whereas after exercising regularly for a few months the amount of glycogen in their muscles can increase to 2g per 100g or more, so their stamina doubles. Other factors such as an increase in blood supply to muscles, an increase in the size and number of energy producing structures within muscle cells (mitochondria), and an increase in muscle bulk

5

will also increase the level of activity you can tolerate. The secret is to start slowly and gradually build up the intensity and length of your exercise period. Ideally you want to end up exercising briskly at least five times per week, and preferably every day. As well as boosting your energy levels – and having a beneficial effect on your love life – this level of exercise will also benefit your heart and circulation as well as your lungs.

Exercise has a number of beneficial effects on physical and emotional health. It can:

- reduce anxiety and tension;
- improve the quality of sleep;
- improve mental energy levels and concentration;
- stimulate release of brain chemicals (endorphins) that reduce pain perception, promote relaxation, and lift your overall mood;
- boost your sex drive.

Taking regular exercise can also prolong your life. A study of more than 10,000 men found that exercise reduced the number of age-related deaths from all causes by almost a quarter – even if exercise was not started until middle age. In particular, deaths from coronary heart disease (CHD) were reduced by over 40 per cent, independent of other risk factors such as overweight, high blood pressure or smoking cigarettes. The likelihood is that women will benefit just as much, too, and will also gain significant benefits on bone health. When a group of post-menopausal women were started on an exercise regime consisting of 5–10 minutes stretching followed by 30 minutes walking, jogging or dance routines, three times a week for one year, their bones were found to be significantly stronger than in a non-exercising control group.

On the physical side, exercise reduces the risk of osteoporosis, has beneficial effects on cholesterol levels and blood pressure, can reduce the risk of a stroke and of developing diabetes, and may also reduce the risk of certain cancers. Unfortunately, only around a quarter of men and women in the UK (across the age range) take enough exercise to reduce their risk of a heart attack.

Exercise that is most beneficial to sexual health is generally high impact in nature (ie, exercise in which activities such as jumping or running increase the impact on your joints) in order to build up strength and stamina. This type of exercise is not always practical in later life. If you have health problems that make exercise difficult, you may find non-weight bearing exercise (eg swimming, cycling) easier than other forms such as walking. If you have a physical disability, your doctor should be willing to refer you for physiotherapy for advice on exercises you can do to help maintain general muscle strength and mobility – even if you are relatively immobile. Some hospitals also provide hydrotherapy so you can exercise in a heated swimming pool under the supervision of a physiotherapist.

Don't overdo it!

The current recommendation is that we should exercise briskly for around 30 minutes, five times a week. Your half hour of exercise doesn't have to be completed all in one go, however, you can divide it into two or three daily sessions of 10–15 minutes if you prefer. Heart specialists in Australia followed 500 older men who either took light exercise on a bicycle, steps and rowing machine with plenty of rests, or who continuously jogged or walked for 30 minutes. After a year, both groups were declared equally fit during treadmill tests. Once you are fit, try to do some form of exercise every day.

People over the age of 70 who are less physically robust can still gain health benefits from any general increase in their level of physical activity. Even standing rather than sitting or lying helps to strengthen bones and activities such as walking, climbing stairs, carrying loads, doing house-work, dancing, DIY and gardening have all been shown to help protect against osteoporotic fractures, for example. It is important, therefore, for older people to maintain their level of physical activity as far as possible. And once you start to feel fitter, and start to notice a general improvement in your body, you will start to feel more attractive too.

Exercise should be an enjoyable part of your life that you look forward to every day – not a chore that you keep putting off and soon forget to do altogether. If you prefer exercising alone, walking (especially brisk walking) in safe areas, cycling, and even gardening are excellent forms of exercise. You could also consider buying a home exercise machine and using it while watching the evening news.

If you prefer companionable exercise, you could borrow a dog for your walks, join a rambling club and take up golf or bowling. If you are keen to try more vigorous exercise, you could join a tennis or badminton club, an aerobics or keep fit class and even take up ballroom dancing.

It is important that your chosen form of exercise can fit into your daily routine so you are most likely to keep it up. This may be early in the morning if you like getting up with the lark, during the day if you are retired or work part-time, or even in the early evening. Only do light exercise (such as walking round the block with the dog) before going to bed, however, otherwise it may interfere with sleep.

If you find it difficult to build an exercise plan into a busy day, try the following:

- walk or cycle short distances instead of taking the car or tube;
- walk up stairs instead of using the lift or escalator;
- try to take a short walk round the block at least once a day;
- if you can't go out, try walking or even running up and down stairs a few times;
- do sit ups, jog on the spot or use a home exercise machine when watching television in the evening;
- walk briskly rather than dawdling whenever possible.

Try also to put more effort into DIY, housework or gardening.

How to start

If you are unfit, start slowly and build up the time and effort you spend on exercise. You should follow these basic safety precautions:

- don't exercise straight after a heavy meal, after drinking alcohol or if you feel unwell;
- always warm up first with a few simple bends and stretches;

- cool down afterwards by walking slowly for a few minutes;
- wear loose clothing and proper footwear where required;
- stop immediately if you feel dizzy, faint, unusually short of breath or develop chest pain.

NB If you are under your doctor's care for any condition (*especially* a heart problem) or are taking medication, seek medical advice before starting a physical exercise programme. Your doctor can guide you about the level of exercise you are likely to be able to tolerate at the start.

Using your pulse rate

Measuring your pulse rate during exercise will ensure you stay within safe levels for burning fat and getting fit without over-stressing your heart. Your pulse is most easily felt:

- on the inner side of your wrist on the same side as your thumb (radial pulse);
- at the side of the neck, under the jaw (carotid pulse).

Count your pulse after sitting quietly for around 15 minutes. This is your resting pulse rate. The heart beats approximately 72 times per minute in the averagely fit person, although some medications (eg beta-blockers) are designed to slow your heart to around 60 beats per minutes to reduce the workload of your heart. Assuming you are not taking any drugs, your resting pulse rate gives a rough assessment of your overall fitness level:

Resting pulse rate (beats per minute)	Level of fitness
60–69	Excellent
70–79	Good
80–85	Fair
86 or over	Room for improvement

To ensure your heart is not being over-stressed, you can take your pulse rate over a 10-second period as a brief check. Assuming you do

9

not have a heart complaint, your level of exercise should be strenuous enough to raise your pulse to the safe 10-second pulse range for your age, to work up a slight sweat, and to make you slightly breathless. Take your 10-second pulse every ten minutes or so during your exercise period – and check it while making love, too. For optimum fitness, ensure your exercising pulse rate stays within the 10-second pulse range for your age, as shown on the following chart:

Age	10-second pulse range
40	18–24
45	18–23
50	17–23
55	17–22
60	16–21
65	15–21
70	15–20
75	14–19
80	14–18

If you are unfit, make sure your pulse stays at the lower end of your 10-second pulse range at first, and slowly work up to the upper end of the range over several months, as and when you feel able to do so.

If at any time your pulse rate goes higher than it should, stop exercising and walk around gently or rest until your pulse falls. When you restart, take things a little more easily.

Try taking your pulse one minute after stopping exercise, too. The more rapidly your pulse rate falls, the fitter you are. After 10 minutes rest, your heart rate should fall to below 100 beats per minute. At the end of 20 minutes exercise, you should feel invigorated rather than exhausted.

The golden rule is, if it hurts – *stop*! If at any time you become so breathless that you can't speak, develop chest tightness or pain, or feel dizzy or unwell, *stop immediately* and seek medical advice.

Stretch exercises to help maintain general suppleness

The following stretch exercises can also help to improve your joint mobility and strengthen your muscles. Repeat them at least 5–10 times, once or twice a day:

Neck stretch

Stand comfortably with feet apart and shoulders relaxed. Slowly drop your left ear towards your left shoulder and hold the stretch for a count of five. Repeat with the right ear.

Shoulders

Stand comfortably, with feet apart. Bend your arms up and clasp your hands behind your head. Pull your elbows forward so they almost touch in front of your chin, then swing your elbows out so they are as wide apart as possible.

Put your arms up behind your back as if trying to fasten your bra (or if you prefer, putting your hands in your back pockets) then lower them again.

Raise your arms above your head, keeping them straight, and stretch as high as you can.

Raise one arm out to your side and slowly swing it around to make a big circle.

Arms

Stand facing a wall, two feet away from it, with your feet a hip-width apart. Keep your back straight, your abdominal muscles pulled in and your pelvis tilted forward. Place your hands flat on the wall, in line with your shoulders, with your fingers pointing up. Do 'push ups' by bending your elbows and leaning in so your nose almost touches the wall – keep your back flat and legs straight. Hold this position briefly then use your arms to push away from the wall. (Breathe in as you bend in, breathe out as you push out.)

11

Wrists

Bend both wrists up and down, side to side and round and round as far as possible.

Fingers

Squeeze a soft foam ball in the palm of your hand by clenching your fingers as tightly as possible. Hold for a count of five, then relax and strengthen your fingers.

Hips

Stand comfortably with feet apart and hands on your hips. Without moving your lower body, rotate your upper body and hips to the right, to the back, to the left and to the front again. Repeat five times in one direction, then five times in the other.

Lie on the floor, with both legs bent so your feet are flat on the floor. Lift one leg up into the air and straighten it. Hold for a count of five. Repeat with the other leg.

NB When straightening one leg, always keep the other knee bent to protect your back. Don't try to lift both legs into the air at the same time.

Legs

Stand comfortably with your back and head straight, tummy tucked in and feet apart. Rest your left hand on a table for support. Bend your left knee slightly, and raise your right leg to grasp your right ankle with your right hand. Keep your knees facing forward. Gently ease your foot in towards your bottom until you feel a mild stretch. Hold for a count of five. Repeat with the other side.

Stand with your back two feet away from a wall, your feet a hip-width apart and your toes pointing forwards. Pull in your abdominal muscles, relax your shoulders, and bend your knees and hips to around 90 degrees, pressing your lower back into the wall. Hold this position for at least 50 seconds.

Stand comfortably with feet apart, knees bent and hands on your knees. Flex your knees up and down, keeping them bent throughout. Don't let your bottom go lower than the level of your knees.

Ankles

Stand comfortably, resting one hand on a table for support. Lift one foot and rotate the ankle in 10 complete circles – first clockwise, then anti-clockwise. Repeat with the other foot.

Stand comfortably, feet slightly apart, with one hand resting on a table for support. Lift both heels up so you are standing on the ball of your foot, then relax down again.

Alcohol

Most people are aware that alcohol can enhance desire but take away performance.

For women, small quantities of alcohol act as an aphrodisiac. After drinking two units of alcohol, female testosterone levels rise steeply one to two hours later. This effect is greatest around the time of ovulation in those who are pre-menopausal. Alcohol does not produce the same testosterone surge in men, however. Unfortunately, in larger quantities alcohol goes on to lower oestrogen levels and female libido, and excessive intake can lead to loss of vaginal secretions, menstrual problems and lowered fertility. In men, any quantity of alcohol can reduce production of testosterone and hasten its conversion to oestrogen in the liver, leading to lowered sperm counts and decreased sex drive. As much as 40 per cent of male sub-fertility has been blamed on just a moderate intake of alcohol alone. Excessive intakes of alcohol in males can lead to impotence, shrunken testicles, a reduction in penis size and loss of pubic hair as a result of underactive testicles. The intakes that can trigger these problems vary from person to person, depending on how an individual's metabolism handles alcohol and how much exercise they take. Sensible drinking levels are no more than 3–4 units of alcohol per day for men, and no more than 2–3 units of alcohol per day for women. Drinking at the upper limit of this range on a regular basis is not advised, and you should ideally aim to have one or two alcohol free days per week. Weekly intakes of over 35 units for women and 50 units for men are considered dangerous.

One unit of alcohol is equivalent to:

- 100 ml (1 glass) of wine; or
- 50 ml (one measure) of sherry; or
- 25 ml (one tot) of spirit; or
- 300 ml (half a pint) of normal strength beer.

If you drink more than the recommended maximum, it is important that you cut back. Milk thistle (widely available in healthfood stores and chemists) is a herb that can help to protect liver cells from the poisonous effects of alcohol and may help to boost testosterone levels where they have been lowered by excess alcohol intake.

Smoking

Smoking cigarettes lowers oestrogen levels in women – enough to bring on the menopause 2–3 years earlier than in non-smokers – and has a long-term detrimental effect on sex drive. In men, smoking ciga-rettes lowers testosterone levels, and there is a direct relationship between levels of arousal and stiffness of erection and number of ciga-rettes smoked. A study of over 300 male smokers measured penile rigidity during nocturnal erections and found a clear, inverse relationship between rigidity and the number of cigarettes smoked each day.

Smoking generates massive amounts of free radicals – harmful by-products of metabolism. These interfere with testicular function and can damage sperm. Smokers use up their vitamin C supplies rapidly and men who smoke 20 or more cigarettes per day have blood vitamin C levels that are up to 40 per cent lower than non-smokers. They also have sperm counts that are 17 per cent lower, reduced sperm motility and a greater percentage of abnormal sperm. Researchers have found that male smokers taking 200mg vitamin C per day can improve their sperm count by as much as 24 per cent, sperm motility by up to 18 per cent and the number of sperm still alive 24 hours after ejaculation by 23 per cent. Sperm are also less likely to clump together, which is the other way in which vitamin C helps to improve sperm quality. Improvement seems to start within a week of increasing vitamin C intake. Vitamin C is found in fruit and vegetables, especially citrus, berry and kiwi fruits.

Healthy diet for a healthy sex life

We are undoubtedly what we eat, so for general health – including sexual health – aim to eat a healthy, wholefood diet:

- always have breakfast to break your overnight fast and provide fuel for energy;
- eat as wide a variety of foods as possible;
- eat fresh, natural, home-made foods rather than convenience, processed foods;
- eat more fresh fruit and vegetables (especially raw ones) containing important vitamins, minerals and antioxidants – aim for a minimum of five servings per day;
- eat more wholegrains, nuts, seeds and pulses;
- eat less red meat and more fish; due to fears of pollution however, we are now advised to eat only two portions of fish per week, including one of oily fish such as salmon, mackerel, herring, sardines. If you wish to eat more fish, select organically farmed salmon or trout;
- drink semi-skimmed or skimmed milk and eat low-fat yoghurt or fromage frais for calcium;
- cut back on your intake of salt and simple sugars;
- avoid cakes, biscuits and fatty, sugary snacks.

Lack of any vitamin or mineral will affect your health and lead to common symptoms such as fatigue, irritability, difficulty concentrating and lowered libido. Vitamins and minerals are vital to your sexual health in a variety of ways, as shown in the table.

Effects of vitamins and minerals on sexual health

Nutrient	Effect on sexual health	Dietary sources
Vitamin A	Helps to regulate sexual growth, development and reproduction	Animal and fish liver, oily fish, dairy products, eggs, butter, margarine. Some carotenoids from fruit and vegetables can be made into vitamin A in the body
B group vitamins	Play a crucial role in the metabolic production of energy, while vitamin B6 regulates sex hormone function	Wholegrains, meat, liver, oily fish, soy, bananas, walnuts, green, leafy vegetables, avocado, egg, yeast extract
Vitamin C	Essential for sperm health and may also help to maintain a healthy prostate gland	Blackcurrants, guava, kiwi fruit, citrus fruit, mangoes, peppers, strawberries, green sprouting vegetables
Vitamin E	Protects sex hormones from oxidation and degradation and is also important for testicular function. Deficiency is linked with a lowered sex drive and reduced fertility	Wheatgerm oil, avocado, butter, margarine, wholegrains, nuts, seeds, oily fish, eggs, broccoli
Calcium	Needed for muscle contraction during orgasm	Milk, cheese, yoghurt, green leafy vegetables, tinned salmon (including bones), nuts, seeds, pulses, white and brown bread, eggs
Magnesium	Needed for sex hormone balance	Seafood, seaweed, meat, eggs, dairy products, wholegrains, soy, nuts, bananas, dark green leafy vegetables
Chromium, copper and manganese	Deficiency linked with lowered sex drive, decreased sperm count and impaired fertility	Eggs, red meat, shellfish, wholegrains, nuts, seeds, vegetables grown in mineral-rich soil
Phosphorus	Necessary for maintaining sexual arousal	Fish, poultry, meat, dairy products, wholegrains, soy, nuts, eggs, yeast extract

Potassium	Improves muscle tone and sexual health. Deficiency can reduce sex drive	Seafood, fruit, vegetables, wholegrains, low-sodium potassium-enriched salts
Iodine	Deficiency causes fatigue and lowered sex drive	Seafood, seaweed, iodised salt, milk, crops grown on soils exposed to sea-spray
Selenium	Essential for the synthesis of hormone-like substances known as prostaglandins (building blocks for sex hormones). Deficiency is linked to lowered sex drive, decreased sperm count and impaired fertility	Brazil nuts, seafood, offal, wholegrains, onions, garlic, broccoli, cabbage, mushrooms, radishes, celery
Zinc	Essential for male sexual health; deficiency reduces testicular function and has been associated with impotence. One of the earliest symptoms of zinc deficiency is reduced taste sensation. Many men are zinc deficient as zinc is so important for male sexual health. Each ejaculate contains around 5mg zinc (one third of a man's daily requirement)	Red meat, seafood (especially oysters), offal, brewer's yeast, wholegrains, pulses, eggs, cheese

More and more people are taking a multivitamin and mineral supplement as a nutritional safety net to safeguard their general and sexual health. As a general rule, it is a good idea to take a product supplying 100 per cent of the recommended daily amount (RDA) for as many micronutrients as possible. Choose a supplement according to your age, as after the age of 50–55, your need for many vitamins and minerals increases. This is partly because your metabolism needs more, and partly because changes in the intestinal wall mean you are less able to absorb certain nutrients from your diet. Those designed for people over the age of 50 will generally contain more antioxidants and B group vitamins, but less iron as body stores of this mineral increase in later life and excess may be harmful.

Sleep

Sleep is a form of unconsciousness that is our natural state of rest. Scientists still do not fully understand how or why we sleep but it is essential for our physical and mental well-being. Sleep is traditionally thought of as a time of rest, rejuvenation and regeneration. As well as allowing muscles and joints to recover from constant use during the day, most of the body's repair work and production of new cells occurs during sleep when growth hormone is secreted in increased amounts.

There are two main types of sleep:

- Rapid eye movement (REM) sleep, in which the eyes are constantly on the move.
- Slow wave (non-REM) sleep, in which the eyes are relatively still.

There are four stages of slow wave sleep: the lightest is stage 1 and the deepest, stage 4. When we first fall asleep, we pass rapidly through stages 1 and 2, then spend 70–100 minutes in stages 3 and 4. Sleep then lightens and a short period of around 10 minutes REM follows. This cycle repeats four to six times throughout the night, but as morning approaches more and more time – up to one hour – is spent in REM sleep.

Interestingly, people who only sleep 5 hours per night get a similar amount of slow wave sleep as those who regularly sleep 8 hours per night. Additional time spent sleeping is spent in REM sleep.

Our sleep pattern naturally changes throughout life, however. As we get older, we spend less and less time in stage 4 (really deep) sleep, so that by the age of 70, most people get no stage 4 sleep at all. Whereas the average younger adult sleeps for 7 hours 12 minutes per night, those aged 70 or more may need as little as 5 hours. As sleep tends to be light, it is common for older people to wake several times during the night, though they may not recall this next morning. Older people are also more likely to take cat-naps during the day, which will reduce the amount of sleep they need at night, too. In fact, we all have a natural tendency to sleep in the afternoon. In parts of Europe, this has evolved into the custom of taking a siesta. Even if you aren't used to taking a siesta, drinking alcohol at lunchtime will accentuate the natural instinct and lead to afternoon drowsiness so this is best avoided if you have sleep problems as it can disrupt your normal sleep pattern.

Insomnia

Insomnia is one of the most common sleep disorders, affecting over five million people in the UK. It is a difficulty in falling asleep, or maintaining sleep, and when you do manage to nod off, the quality of sleep is not restorative. Most people have suffered from insomnia at some stage of their life – usually when they are worried or stressed. Insomnia has a significant effect on quality of life. People suffering from insomnia report higher levels of stress, anxiety, depression and physical illness and have greater relationship, sexual and occupational problems than those who regularly enjoy a good night's sleep. Insomnia and daytime sleepiness also affect safety and performance, and can double the chance of experiencing an accident while operating machinery or driving a car. Recurrent lack of sleep leads to poor performance and achievement during the day. It is also linked with increased risk of serious illness such as high blood pressure, stroke and even a heart attack.

Insomnia may be:

- transient – lasting a few days, eg jetlag;
- short term – lasting 1–3 weeks, eg stress, bereavement;
- long term – lasting over 3 months related to anxiety, depression or other medical problems that can interfere with sleep such as pain (eg arthritis, indigestion), prostate problems, breathing problems (eg congestive heart failure, asthma, bronchitis, emphysema), dry itchy skin.

19

Snoring

Snoring can cause sleep problems for the person affected and their bed partner. Snoring occurs when the airway partially collapses, blocking the inflow of oxygen and the outflow of waste carbon dioxide gas. If the airway becomes completely obstructed, breathing can stop for ten seconds or more. This is known as sleep apnoea. Failure to breathe causes a build up of carbon dioxide in the blood which eventually triggers breathing again. As the airway is jerked open, a gasp occurs and the sufferer may briefly wake up. In extreme cases, this can happen as often as 1000 times per night resulting in the daytime symptoms of sleeplessness. Sleep apnoea is thought to affect 5 per cent of the population. Most sufferers are middle aged or older males who smoke cigarettes and have a collar size greater than 17, but it can occur in women and slim men, too, if the airways are particularly slack.

People with sleep apnoea are not aware of having a problem – especially if they sleep alone – but it can cause symptoms such as:

■   morning headache;
■   waking up feeling drunk (even though no alcohol has been taken);
■   waking up with a frightening sensation of choking and fighting for air;
■   excessive daytime sleepiness and yawning;
■   falling asleep during the day;
■   poor memory;
■   lack of concentration with thoughts petering out mid-sentence;
■   deteriorating driving skills and increased risk of accidents.

If you think you may have sleep apnoea, seek medical advice as it can be treated in a number of ways to help stop the soft palate from collapsing and vibrating. Self-help includes:

■   losing any excess weight;
■   avoiding alcohol and cigarettes;
■   avoiding sleeping tablets as these make the problem worse;
■   getting plenty of sleep – go to bed as early as possible;

- sewing a pouch containing a cork or walnut into the back of your pyjamas or nightie, to prevent you lying on your back;
- raising the head of the bed 10cm to help stop your tongue flopping backwards;
- using special anti-snoring pillows.

Tips to help you get a good night's sleep

- Avoid napping during the day as this will make it more difficult to sleep at night.
- Take regular exercise, as active people tend to sleep more easily.
- Avoid strenuous exercise late in the evening as this will keep you awake.
- Try to eat your evening meal before 6 pm and resist late night snacks, especially of rich food.
- Avoid over-indulgence in substances that interfere with sleep such as caffeine (coffee, tea, chocolate, colas) nicotine and alcohol – although alcohol may help you fall asleep, you are likely to have a disturbed sleep once the drugged effect has worn off.
- Take time to unwind from the stresses of the day before going to bed – read a book, listen to soothing music or have a candlelit bath.
- A warm, milky drink just before going to bed will help you to relax – hot milk with cinnamon or nutmeg is better than chocolate drinks that contain some caffeine.
- Don't drink too much fluid in the evening – a full bladder is guaranteed to disturb your rest.
- Get into a habit by going to bed at a regular time each night and getting up at the same time each morning.
- Set a bed-time routine such as checking house security, brushing your teeth, bathing and setting the alarm clock to set the mood for sleep.
- Make sure your bed is comfortable, and your bedroom warm, dark and quiet – noise and excessive cold or heat will keep you awake. A temperature of 18–24 degrees Celsius is ideal.

- If you can't sleep, don't lie there tossing and turning. Get up and read or watch the television for a while. If you are worried about something, write down all the things on your mind and promise yourself you will deal with them in the morning, when you are feeling fresher. When you feel sleepy, go back to bed and try again. If sleep does not come within 15 minutes, get up and repeat this process.
- Preserve your bedroom as a place for sleep (and making love) – don't use it for eating, working or watching television.
- Check with a pharmacist whether any prescribed (or over-the-counter) medication you are taking can interfere with sleep. Common culprits include beta blockers, oral decongestants, theophylline and steroids.

Natural sleep remedies

Valerian is one of the most effective herbal remedies for stress, anxiety and insomnia. A pharmacy-only standardised extract called Sedonium has been licensed by the Medicines Control Agency for sleep disorders, anxiety and stress. Clinical trials in both Germany and the UK have shown that Sedonium (600mg taken 30–60 minutes before bedtime) improves the ability to fall asleep and the onset and development of deep, short-wave sleep. It is also effective for mild anxiety when taken at a dose of 600mg up to three times daily. Valerian is non-addictive and acts in a different way to sleeping drugs (see below). Ask your pharmacist for further details – check there are no interactions if you wish to try it but are taking prescribed medications or other over-the-counter treatments.

Homeopathy

If your mind is over-active, try Coffea 30c. For sleeplessness leaving you irritable and unrefreshed, try Nux vomica 30c. If you are overtired and can't get comfortable, try Arnica 30c. Take half an hour before going to bed and repeat every half hour if necessary.

Aromatherapy

Enjoy a soothing aromatherapy bath containing lavender, mandarin, lemon or camomile oils – or sprinkle a few drops on a hankie and tuck it under your pillow.

Sleeping tablets

If left untreated, sleep problems can have a serious effect on quality of life. The long-term use of sleeping tablets is no longer recommended, but a short, sharp course (2–4 weeks) can sometimes get you back into a sleep routine where insomnia is severe, disabling or extremely distressing. Newer sleeping tablets (eg zaleplon, zolpidem, zopiclone) preserve the normal pattern of sleep and, as they have less effect on REM and other stages of sleep, are less likely to leave a hangover effect next morning. Sonata (zaleplon) is interesting as it belongs to a new class of drug, the pyrazolopyrimidines, and is structurally different from all other hypnotic agents currently available. It starts to work very quickly (ie in around 30 minutes), maintains the natural pattern of sleep (so that the time spent in each stage of sleep is similar to that seen with placebo) and has a short half-life which means it is rapidly cleared from the circulation. It is therefore the first hypnotic to be licensed for use 'as required' throughout the night, and can either be taken at bedtime, or later (eg up until two or three in the morning) as long as there are still four hours potential sleep remaining. It also seems to produce fewer residual hangover effects, less rebound insomnia and fewer withdrawal symptoms than some other sleeping pills.

While the regular use of hypnotic drugs is discouraged, they can have an important clinical role in treating short-term or intermittent insomnia in people who have difficulty falling asleep and your doctor may be happy to prescribe them short term. Older sleeping tablets (eg nitrazepam, flurazepam) are not a good idea as they interfere with the normal sleep pattern and damp down the amount of REM sleep you get. This causes day-time drowsiness and can lead to rebound insomnia (in which difficulty sleeping returns, and is sometimes even worse then before, when the treatment is stopped). This type of treatment is also more likely to cause withdrawal symptoms.

I usually advise people to avoid over-the-counter sleep medications containing antihistamines. Some of these have been shown in sleep laboratories to give a poor night's sleep with an abnormal sleep pattern, leaving you drowsy the next day and more prone to accidents.

Relaxation techniques

You cannot hope to enjoy a healthy and fulfilling sex life if you are stressed, tired and overworked – these are common causes of low sex drive and poor erections. Try to avoid stressful situations, make time for relaxation and ensure plenty of sleep.

A wide range of relaxation therapies are available, according to your mood and needs. Touch therapies such as acupressure, shiatsu, aromatherapy massage and reflexology are beneficial, while yoga and meditation help you learn how to exert mind control over the physical responses of your body so you feel more in control.

Meditation is an art that uses the ability to empty your mind of all thoughts so you can direct all senses inwards. With practice, it is possible to maintain a level of spiritual awareness and tranquillity that transcends everyday life. Useful techniques to achieve a meditative state involve initially focusing your thoughts on a single, abstract image or a low pitched hum or phrase known as a mantra.

Relaxation exercise: mantra meditation

Choose a warm, quiet room, draw the curtains and light a soft lamp or a few candles. Take off your shoes and loosen your clothing. Sit or lie down in a comfortable position and concentrate on listen to a relaxation tape – either classical music or natural Earth sounds such as running water, jungle noises, bird song or sea sounds (you can make your own, or buy one of the many relaxation tapes available). As you listen, repeat a personal calming mantra such as 'om' or 'calm' quietly to yourself. Tune into your breathing and feel the tension in your muscles slowly drift away. As you listen to the sound, imagine your body become increasingly weightless until you find yourself floating among clouds, bathed in warming sunlight. Repeat your mantra in your mind as you become more and more relaxed, so it becomes your cue to relaxation. In future times of stress, imagine the melodies of the relaxation tape in your mind and repeat your personal mantra to help stress slip away.

Whole body relaxation

Find somewhere quiet, warm and semi-dark to lie down. Remove your shoes and loosen tight clothing. Keep your eyes closed throughout the session.

First, lift your arms into the air, bending them at the elbow. Clench your fists hard and concentrate on the tension in these muscles. Breathe in deeply and slowly. As you breathe out, start to relax and let the tension in your arms drain away. Release your clenched fists and lower your arms gently beside you. Feel the tension flow out of them until your fingers start to tingle.

Now shrug your shoulders as high as you can. Feel the tension in your head, shoulders, neck and chest. Hold for a moment, then slowly let the tension flow away as you continue breathing gently and slowly.

Lift your head and push it forwards while tightening your facial muscles. Clench your teeth, frown and screw up your eyes. Hold this tension for a few seconds then gradually start to relax.

Continue in this way, working through the remaining muscles in your back, abdomen, buttocks and legs. Make sure tension does not creep back into the parts of your body you have already relaxed. A feeling of warmth should wash over the areas you have relaxed and your body should feel heavy relaxed. Breathe calmly and slowly as you feel all that tension drain away.

Imagine you are lying in a warm, sunny meadow with a stream bubbling gently beside you. Relax for at least 20 minutes, occasionally checking your body for tension.

Activating your inner smile

A lovely Chinese technique called 'the inner smile' only takes a few minutes and brings rapid relaxation and rejuvenation to help leave stress behind.

Sit comfortably with your back straight and your arms relaxed at your side. Imagine something that makes you smile, and start to smile internally so it is felt by you only – it doesn't have to be visible. Let the smile shine out of your eyes and travel inwards, so that it spreads all over your body before concentrating just below the navel. As your smile radiates within, it will generate a feeling of relaxation and calm. Once you feel relaxed, you can return to normal activity enriched by feelings of warmth, harmony and inner strength.

2 Loving in Later Life

Making love is a physical expression of the depth of your feelings for your partner. In a long term relationship, the richness of lovemaking is built on foundations of knowledge, trust and deep understanding. The emotions you feel before, during and after sex can enhance your lovemaking and bring you closer together. These feelings of intimacy can extend throughout your whole relationship and even guide your selection of clothes and scent based on what you know your partner likes. Show your feelings by giving love tokens such as chocolates, perfume and flowers – these are seen as important at the beginning of a relationship but are just as precious when used to show love and affection in later years. Small, spontaneous yet carefully selected presents show someone you have been thinking of them because you care – not just because there is an anniversary or birthday to celebrate.

Variation is the secret of keeping desire alive in later life. In a long-term relationship, sex can easily become routine, yet with a little effort you can keep your love life fresh and exciting. Learn to surprise each other so you never quite know what to expect next.

Getting in the mood

However busy you are, it is important to find time to relax together and to create an atmosphere conducive to romance. Mood music, flickering candles and sensual, aromatherapy oils that scent the air will help set the scene. Many couples who have been together for a while undress themselves and meet up in bed, already naked, or wearing nightie and pyjamas. They then miss out on the pleasures of slowly undressing each other while kissing and fondling, or using candlelight to add to the sensuality of the experience.

Setting the scene

Make sure that wherever you choose to make love is private, with no possibility of being disturbed by family, carers or others living in your home. If necessary, put a lock on the bedroom door. The room should be at a comfortable temperature, so you can lie down uncovered without feeling unduly cold. Try to ensure the lighting is subdued – flickering candlelight or firelight is ideal, but make sure the flames are safely enclosed. Many couples enjoy taking a candlelit bath together first, soaping each other down with lots of bubbles, and indulging in a glass or two of wine. Alcohol is excellent for lowering your inhibitions but don't over-indulge as excess will impair your performance.

Being spontaneous

Many couples only make love in the bedroom after retiring for the night. If the mood takes you, however, why not make love wherever you are in the house – on the kitchen table, in the bathroom, on the living room floor, or on the stairs.

Making love in a warm bath with plenty of bubbles – or in the shower – can be highly erotic. This gives you the opportunity to soap each other down in intimate places. Take care not to slip, however, especially if either of you is frail.

Some couples prefer to lock the doors and pull the curtains; for others, half the excitement comes from the risk of being discovered. Making love outdoors can be exciting for some – whether it be on a windswept sand dune, in a moonlit field, or against a sunny tree. In these situations, however, you do need to be confident that you won't be disturbed or charged with a breach of the peace.

Making time for sex

To enjoy foreplay at its best, it is important to set aside enough time. Few people will feel fulfilled by a sexual encounter consisting of a quick introductory fumble followed by a few minutes of thrusting. Ideally, you need to allow at least an hour to enjoy better sex – especially in later life when sexual responses may not be as quick and reliable as they once were. Choose a time when you are both refreshed, rather than tired at the end of a busy and demanding day. If you are used to making love late at night after going to bed, try making love in the afternoon or early evening instead. Many older people find the morning is the best time for them, especially as men often wake up with a morning erection that is firmer than those achieved later in the day.

Foreplay

Foreplay – the touching and caressing two people enjoy to bring themselves to full sexual arousal – is important if both partners are to obtain optimum enjoyment from love-making. For a man, lack of good foreplay may mean that his erection does not become fully hard, that he will take longer to ejaculate or may not reach orgasm at all. For woman, lack of foreplay usually means she will not produce enough natural lubrication to ensure that penetration is comfortable for both partners. Lack of foreplay also means a woman is less likely to reach orgasm. It usually takes a woman longer to be aroused than a man, and she will need a lot of clitoral stimulation to reach her climax. This may require patience and some skill on the part of her partner.

Foreplay health checks

A couple can contribute to each other's sexual health by regularly examining the other's breasts or testicles as a normal part of foreplay. This can help to detect breast or testicular cancer at an early, treatable stage. If you notice any lumps or irregularity, tell your partner *after* you've finished making love and encourage them to seek medical

29

advice as soon as possible. Try not to panic. Many non-serious types of lump can also occur in the breasts and testicles, but all should be investigated, just to be on the safe side.

Testicles

According to Cancer Research UK, nearly 1,900 men are diagnosed with testicular cancer each year. The good news is that treatment is highly effective and most testicular cancers can be cured if caught early enough. The most common symptom is swelling in part of one testicle. This is usually painless, although some men notice an ache or heaviness. It is advisable for any man to check his testicles regularly for lumps – or, alternatively, his partner can check them for him as part of foreplay.

- Hold each testicle gently between the thumb and fingertips of both hands.
- Slowly bring the thumb and fingertips of one hand together whilst relaxing the fingertips of the other. Alternate this action so the testicle glides smoothly between both sets of fingers. This lets you assess the shape and texture of the testicle – you may be able to feel a soft tube (epididymis) attached towards the top, at the back, which is normal.
- Repeat with the other testicle.

Each testicle should feel soft and smooth – like a hard-boiled egg without its shell.

Breasts

One in nine women will eventually develop breast cancer. The first sign of this is often a lump which is likely to be discovered by either the woman herself, or by her partner. All women should aim to be 'breast aware' which includes knowing how their own breasts feel while in the bath, shower or dressing. Some breasts are naturally more lumpy than others but subtle changes can be detected. The breasts can also be fondled and examined – either by the woman or her partner – during foreplay. As well as helping to arouse both partners, this also gives an opportunity for detecting any lumps that may need investigation and treatment. It is also important that women accept invitations for screening mammography which helps to detect breast cancer early. Ask your doctor for details.

Breast Awareness Five Point Code

- Know what is normal for you;

- Look and feel;

- Know what changes to look for;

- Report any changes without delay;

- Attend for breast screening if you are aged 50 or over.

Signs to look out for include:

- Any change in the outline or shape of the breasts. Moving and lifting the arms will help you detect these.
- Any skin changes such as puckering or dimpling over a breast.
- Any discomfort or pain that is different from normal – especially if it keeps recurring.
- Any lumps, thickening or bumpiness in one breast or armpit – especially if this is new or different from the other side.
- Any change in a nipple, including change in position, turning inwards, unusual discharge, bleeding or a rash that does not heal easily.

It is important to remember that men can get breast cancer too (although it is much rarer in men than in women). So any such changes in a male partner's breast should also prompt an immediate visit to the doctor.

Erogenous zones

It helps to know the parts of your partner's body that are sensitive to stimulation and which promote sexual arousal. These areas, known as erogenous zones, can be stimulated by gentle stroking, licking, blowing or nibbling. The major erogenous zones – lips, nipples, buttocks, breasts and external genitals – are the same in most people. The secondary erogenous zones vary from person to person, and can include the back of the neck, the eyelids, ears and earlobes plus the soft skin at the top of the inner thighs. Most people are also very sensitive around the anus, but be careful. Although this sensation is pleasurable for some, others find it distinctly uncomfortable or even unpleasant. Working out where your own erogenous zones are situated – and finding those of your partner – is half the fun of making love.

Stimulating the erogenous zones

The erogenous zones can be stimulated by gentle fondling, squeezing, sucking or even biting (as long as you are careful!). Gently nibbling the earlobes is a turn-on for some, whilst others find blowing on the back of the neck, stroking the inner thighs, licking behind the knees or having their toes sucked more erotic. These sensitive areas also like being wetted then blown dry, stimulated by a vibrator (see page 49), or lightly touched by a melting ice cube. Erogenous zones respond especially well to lashings of lubrication – apply body lotions, massage oil or even favourite foods such as dripping chocolate sauce or ice-cream. If foreplay is likely to become messy, protect bed covers with towels. Or vary the venue and make love in the shower, bathroom, or even the kitchen as long as you know you won't be disturbed.

To add an extra dimension to foreplay, try sucking an ice cube before kissing your partner somewhere intimate. Try a little spearmint toothpaste under the foreskin for extra stimulation. Experiment with the feel of different textures such as velvets, fur, silk, leather or feathers against sensitive skin.

Lips

As well as using the lips, tongue and teeth to gently kiss, lick and nibble your partner's erogenous zones, remember that the lips themselves are sensitive – especially on the inside and on the outer, surrounding skin.

Nipples

The nipples contain sensitive nerve endings and become erect in both sexes during arousal. The pigmented area surrounding the nipples – the areolae – sometimes swells enough to look bruised. These delicate structures usually require gentle, sensitive handling, but some people prefer slightly rougher fondling, squeezing and sucking. Experiment to see which sensations your partner prefers, and whether one nipple is more sensitive than another.

Breasts

The female breasts become filled with blood during sexual excitement and may swell slightly as she becomes aroused. Most women enjoy having their breasts massaged with sensual aromatherapy oils or lotions. Using edible oils (eg walnut), fruit-flavoured gels or cream means you can continue kissing the nipples afterwards.

Buttocks

Slowly massaging the buttocks and lightly trailing the fingers down towards the soft, inner thighs, or following the curve down towards the anus can be a sensual experience for both of you.

Female external genitals

The female external genitals – including the folds of skin (labia) surrounding the vaginal entrance – are highly sensitive. The clitoris is the most sensitive female erogenous zone. It is 2–3cm long and sits above the entrance to the vagina where the lips meet at the top. Usually, it is retracted and hidden away but when a woman is sexually aroused, her clitoris swells, lengthens and becomes more prominent. Many women prefer not to be touched in these exquisitely sensitive areas until they are fully aroused. It then becomes one of the most important erogenous zones. Direct stimulation of the clitoris should be gentle and sensitive, with plenty of lubrication – dry or rough handling can produce unpleasant sensations. Most women find it uncomfortable for the clitoris to be stroked upwards as this can irritate the urethral opening beneath. So, when stroking the clitoris, use a downward action (from the pubic hair down towards the vagina). Try making gentle round-and-round motions to one side of the clitoris using two or three fingers. Alternatively, use your palm or the flats of your fingers to stimulate the entire area using a slow circular motion. Most women enjoy being penetrated by one finger while their clitoris is being stimulated – as long as the partner's fingernails are short. During intercourse, penile thrusting often only indirectly stimulates the clitoris by stretching surrounding tissues so using positions which enhance clitoral stimulation (see page 45) or the bridge manoeuvre (see page 40) in which direct stimulation of the clitoris brings the female to the brink of orgasm which is then triggered by penetration.

Male external genitals

The male external genitals – penis and scrotum – are extremely sensitive, especially the rim around the head of the penis (glans) and the fold of skin (frenulum) at the back of the glans. The root of the penis where it passes beneath the scrotum and back towards the anus is also very sensitive and often overlooked as an erogenous zone when making love. Some sexual positions allow the man's partner to reach down and massage the area between his scrotum and anus (perineum) which can be highly exciting for a man while he is thrusting.

Sensual massage

Giving your partner a sensual massage is a lovely way to start foreplay. Use a specially formulated massage lotion – one containing sensual aromatherapy oils is ideal.

Giving and receiving an aromatherapy massage is a relaxing, pleasurable experience. Massage your partner for 30 minutes, then relax while the touch experience is returned.

- Choose a firm surface such as lying on several towels spread on the floor.
- Make sure the room is warm with gentle light and slow, relaxing background music.

- Warm the massage oil or lotion by placing the bottle in a bowl of comfortably hot water. Alternatively, rub some oil in your hands to warm it before using.
- Ask your partner to lie on his or her front, and cover them with a large bath towel. Expose the area you are working on and cover them again before moving on.
- Begin with long, flowing, simple strokes over their back from shoulder to waist, to warm the skin. Then, vary the pressure and length of stroke you use, keeping movements flowing and rhythmic with one hand in contact with their body at all times. Try alternating firm movements with feathery ones.
- When your partner is relaxed, gently smooth massage lotion into the lower back and work down to the buttocks and backs of the legs. Use slow, fluid motions and if you find a muscle that seems knotted or tense, concentrate on that area with gentle kneading movements.
- Don't worry if you feel awkward at first – you will soon improve with practice.
- Ask your partner what they like and be alert for appreciative noises.

When you've finished with the back, ask your partner to turn over.

- Massage the chest and shoulders – but avoid the breasts in women, at first.
- Slowly work your way down to the abdomen and then the front of the legs.
- Stroke towards the heart and if you are going to stop here, finish by holding your partner's feet for a few seconds as this helps to 'ground' them.
- If you want to be more intimate, you can move on to the breasts/chest and massage the insides of your partner's thighs.
- Try alternating firm movements with feathery ones, slowly working your way – if you both wish – towards the genitals.
- Use soft, slow and gentle strokes with plenty of lubrication.

NB Do not apply aromatherapy essential oils directly to the genitals, even when diluted.

By now, you should both be fairly aroused. You now need to decide whether you want to enjoy an orgasm without penetration, whether you would like to change roles, with your partner starting to massage you, or whether to progress to full intercourse. Don't feel you have to race towards penetrative sex. A session of mutual masturbation can be equally enjoyable for both of you.

The normal sexual response

The sexual response can be separated into four separate stages. In the first, known as the *excitement phase*, sexual interest is aroused through a variety of stimuli such as sight, smell, touch and emotional feelings. In men, this is usually when erection occurs as blood floods into the penis (see Chapter 6). The excitement phase lasts an average of 15 minutes in women, while in men it is usually much shorter, lasting less than 5 minutes, as they move on more quickly to the next stage of sexual arousal, which is known as the *plateau phase*.

The plateau phase is a stage of higher arousal in which the heart rate speeds up and blood pressure rises. Breathing becomes more rapid and you may also start to perspire. One in four people develop a distinctive sexual flush as blood vessels just beneath the skin dilate. When flushing occurs, it tends to start on the lower abdomen or chest and can spread to the neck, face and limbs. The nipples become more erect – especially in women – and in men the skin of the scrotum thickens and contracts. The testicles draw up towards the base of the penis and may increase in volume by as much as 50 per cent due to congestion with blood. During sexual arousal, the vaginal tissues become increasingly engorged and change in colour from rosy pink to purplish red. The upper two thirds of the vagina lengthen and balloon outwards, and the uterus is pulled up, producing an intense desire for penetration. At the same time, the entrance to the vagina pouts downwards and the lower third of the vagina thickens to grip the penis more tightly. The thickness of the end of the penis also increases to improve friction and lubricating fluid is released in both sexes.

The plateau phase lasts an average of 15 minutes in men, and results in an overpowering urge to thrust. In women, the plateau phase is shorter – around 5 minutes. However, this phase can be prolonged to 30 minutes or longer to heighten and intensify sexual sensations in both sexes. When sexual intercourse takes place, the thrusting action of the penis increases arousal level still further, and the physical changes occurring during the plateau phase become more intense until the participants experience a feeling that orgasm is inevitable. In women, orgasm can be delayed at any time by external distractions such as the phone ringing. In men, however, there is a build up of secretions within the tube running through the prostate gland, to a point at which ejaculation becomes inevitable.

The third stage of the sexual response is *orgasm* itself. Orgasm is an intensely pleasurable sensation that is difficult to define – some feel it emanating from their head, some from the genitals while others feel it 'everywhere' at the same time. During orgasm, nerve impulses spread via the pudendal nerves (nerves in the genital area) and cause rhythmic, wave-like contractions of the pelvic floor muscles and sometimes of the thigh muscles as well. Contractions usually last 3–10 seconds and only rarely last longer than 15 seconds. During orgasm, a number of brain chemicals are released, heart rate and blood pressure peak and hyperventilation is common.

The final stage of sexual arousal, known as *resolution*, then follows, in which the heart rate, blood pressure and genital blood return to their resting levels. In females resolution is gradual with breasts, nipples and genitals taking as long as 30 minutes to return to normal. Resolution occurs more rapidly in the male, taking only a few minutes as long as orgasm has occurred. If the plateau phase does not end in orgasm, however, resolution may take several hours to complete. This results in pelvic congestion and heavy, dragging sensations which can be uncomfortable.

Refractory period

After a successful male orgasm, there is a time – known as the absolute refractory period – in which further orgasm is impossible. This is probably related to the high circulating levels of adrenaline and activation of inhibitory centres in the brain. In young males, the refractory period is short, often only a few minutes. After middle age it usually lasts at least 20 minutes, and often longer. In older males it may last several hours or more. Females do not experience a refractory period so multiple orgasms can occur more easily.

Afterplay

Afterplay is just as important as foreplay and penetration – especially for women. Holding her close, caressing her gently and telling her how much you enjoyed your love-making will help her to feel comfortable, respected, safe and loved.

Communication

For a satisfactory sex life it is vital that both partners communicate with each other when making love. This can mean whispering, talking, giving simple words of encouragement or a gentle message to stop and try something else. Your processes of sexual arousal are finally tuned – you need to be able to interpret each other's responses to know when you are doing something your partner likes and, equally, when you are doing something they are less keen on. Let your partner know where you like being touched – either by telling them, or by taking their fingers in yours and showing them what to do. It can sometimes be difficult and embarrassing to say things like 'harder', 'faster', 'softer', 'yes, just like that' or 'slower' but these are an important part of achieving a better sex life – for both of you. Some people are able to get these messages across by the tone and pitch of their moans. If you are unsure what your partner is trying to tell you, however, always ask. A whispered 'Is that good?' or 'Do you want me to stop?' will usually get you back on track.

Simultaneous orgasms

Many couples consider that reaching sexual climax together is the height of better sex. To achieve simultaneous orgasms, you need to know your partner's sexual responses as well as your own to gauge how quickly their excitement is mounting. Once you know your partner is approaching orgasm, from a pre-arranged signal for example, you can let yourself go. Some men find that their partner's muscular contractions during orgasm are enough to trigger their own climax and vice versa.

Delaying orgasm

By deliberately delaying your climax during the plateau stage of orgasm, the sensations felt during climax are usually more intense. This is due to increased pelvic congestion, a build up of secretions in the male and more intense contractions in both partners.

Men can delay their orgasm by prolonging foreplay and the excitement phase of orgasm to maintain sexual tension for as long as possible. Extra time spent on foreplay will also help the female partner reach a higher level of arousal. Once penetration has occurred, the male can continue fine-tuning his approach to orgasm by slowing down or stopping thrusting when he feels ejaculation is imminent – but before it becomes inevitable. Another technique for delaying orgasm is to gently pull the testicles back down into the scrotum when they rise up to the base of the penis when fully aroused – but be careful not to twist them. You can also use the 'squeeze' technique – originally developed to help men with premature ejaculation (see page 127) – in which either partner firmly squeezes the man's penis between thumb and two fingers just below the ridge where the top of the penis (glans, or 'helmet') joins the shaft. Squeeze firmly for five seconds, then wait for a minute before resuming sex. This technique can be repeated as often as you wish.

For women who take a long time to reach climax, these delaying tactics will increase the chance of her having an orgasm during penetration, especially if her partner can reach down and provide some clitoral stimulation, too. According to experts, foreplay prolonged for a minimum of 20 minutes, and thrusting sustained for a minimum of 15 minutes is usually sufficient for the majority of women to climax. Delaying orgasm is something a woman can try, too.

Few women are able to achieve orgasm during the thrusting action of intercourse itself – this is perfectly normal and no reflection on the skills of either of you as a lover. Some research suggests that women may need as much as 20 minutes foreplay before penetration occurs in order to reach sexual climax. In fact, 8 per cent of adult women have never experienced an orgasm, even when masturbating, and many more do not experience one until they have been sexually active for several years.

The bridge manoeuvre

Many women find it difficult to achieve orgasm during penetrative sex alone. If a woman can have an orgasm during foreplay, however, a technique known as 'the bridge manoeuvre' can help her to climax during intercourse as well. The man directly stimulates his partner's clitoris with his lubricated fingers during foreplay. As soon as she feels that orgasm is inevitable, she lets him know by some prearranged signal (eg saying 'now'). He then immediately inserts his penis into her vagina and *slowly* thrusts up and down. This is often enough to trigger her orgasm. At first, she may need continued clitoral stimulation with his hand, too. This is most easily done if you both lie curled side by side, facing the same way. The female partner bends up the knee of her uppermost leg and drops it backwards so that it rests over the male as he lies behind her. He should then be able to reach over and gently stimulate her clitoris with one hand while inserting his penis from behind. Some women prefer penetration only to occur at the point of climax, others prefer to feel their partner inside them from the beginning, using this position.

Penis size

It is important to cover this topic as many men worry about the size of their penis – especially if they have noticed their genitals shrinking slightly in later life. A normal penis can be any size or shape as long as it is anatomically able to penetrate the female partner. Nine out of ten men have a penis that measures between 14.5cm (5.6 in) and 17.5cm (7 in) when erect, but the penis can shrink a little in later life if testosterone levels fall or ability to respond to testosterone reduces. This does not matter, as penis size is less important to a woman than many men think. There is no relation between penis size and a man's ability to be a caring and considerate lover. His qualities as a lover – patience, generosity and lovingness – contribute more to a woman's experience of good sex than her partner's size. It is stimulation of the clitoris, which lies outside the vagina, which triggers the female orgasm – and this is possible whatever the size of her partner's penis. In fact, many women prefer a slightly smaller penis to a larger one. A small penis is more likely to stimulate the clitoris by repeatedly entering and disengaging from the vagina during sex. Similarly, no man need worry that he is too big for his partner – the female vagina can expand enough to allow birth of a baby. If you are on the large side however, you need to ensure there is plenty of lubrication. Research suggests that a penis which is thicker than normal at the base may be able to stimulate the female clitoris more easily. A man with a thin penis need not worry however. A study using an ultrasound probe to measure movement of the female clitoris during vaginal intercourse found this was best if a man entered his partner from behind, with the female lying on her side. This was true, whatever the size of the man's penis.

Pelvic floor exercises

Strengthening the pelvic floor muscles helps to give both partners more control during orgasm. Pelvic floor exercises are beneficial for both men and women and can produce more prolonged, intense sensations.

41

Females

The vagina is surrounded by pelvic floor muscles that grip the penis when making love. Research suggests that as many as 40 per cent of women lack normal tone in their pelvic floor muscles. This can interfere with sexual pleasure and lead to urinary leakage known as stress incontinence (see Chapter 5).

Health specialists recommend that every woman aged 16 and over should practise pelvic floor exercises for ten minutes a day. As well as improving urinary control, toning your pelvic floor muscles helps to tighten the vaginal muscles and strengthen contractions during orgasm. Improving the strength and flexibility of these muscles will also make sexual positions such as squatting on top of your partner easier and more comfortable. You will also be able to grip your partner more firmly when he is inside you, which will increase sexual pleasure for you both.

For general toning up of pelvic muscles and to reduce congestion, try the following three exercises. They are best performed after a bath or shower when you are warm and relaxed.

Pelvic gyration

- Stand with your feet apart and your knees slightly bent. Place your hands on your hips, jut your bottom out and rotate your pelvis slowly in a clockwise direction.
- Continue rotating your pelvis round to form a complete circle that is as wide as possible.
- Continue these pelvic gyrations for 1–2 minutes, then gyrate your pelvis round in an anti-clockwise direction for another 1–2 minutes.

Simple pelvic floor exercise

Next, learn the following pelvic floor exercises and practice them for at least five minutes once or twice a day. A simple exercise is to pull up your front and back passages tightly as if trying to stop your bowels from opening. Hold tight for a count of four and repeat this every quarter of an hour.

Advanced pelvic floor exercises

A more advanced pelvic floor exercise is to stand with your feet wide apart, and to squat right down so that your knees are bent, and your bottom is just off the floor. Rest your fingers or palms on the floor between your feet, and let your buttocks drop down as far as possible. Breathe in deeply, then breathe out, letting your back passage and pelvic floor muscles relax. Then breathe in four or five short breaths without exhaling in between. With each breath in, draw up and tighten your pelvic floor muscles as if pulling up your vagina step by step. Then breathe out five times slowly (without inhaling in between) and release your pelvic floor muscles in short steps. Repeat ten times.

Finally, for women who don't mind touching themselves, another pelvic floor exercise you could try is to insert two fingers inside your vagina and try to squeeze them by contracting and tightening your vaginal muscles. Once you are adept at this, you can practice squeezing your partner when making love, too.

Males

Men can also tone up their pelvic floor muscles to release tension and congestion. These exercises are best performed after a bath or shower when you are warm and relaxed.

Finding the muscles

The easiest way for males to identify their pelvic floor muscles is to start urinating, then concentrate on stopping the flow mid-stream (NB women should not do this as it may increase the risk of bladder infection in females). Practice this every time you visit the bathroom until you are able to accurately squeeze these muscles at will and can start exercising them regularly. Start with ten quick squeezes, holding each one for the count of three. Repeat two or three times a day. Build up to 20 quick squeezes at a time, holding each for the count of three. After around a month, add in five long, slow squeezes after your 20 quick squeezes. Squeeze in to a count of ten, then hold for a count of ten. When you are comfortable with these, build up to ten long, slow squeezes after each series of 20 quick squeezes.

Exercises to relieve pelvic tension

■ Stand with your feet apart and your knees slightly bent. Hold your arms by your side with your palms facing forwards. Breathe in deeply and pull your pelvis back. As you breathe out, let your pelvis rock forward and arms, hands and genitals move upwards. Repeat in a smooth, continuous motion for two minutes.

■ Stand with your feet apart and your knees slightly bent. Place your hands on your hips, jut your bottom out and rotate your pelvis slowly in a clockwise direction. Continue rotating your pelvis round to form a complete circle that is as wide as possible. Continue for one minute, then switch to a similar, anti-clockwise direction for another minute.

■ The Chinese believe that squeezing the prostate gland increases secretion of sex hormones and reduces congestion. You can do this while sitting, standing or lying, whichever you prefer. Squeeze your anal muscles together tightly and hold for as long as is comfortable. Relax for a minute or two then repeat as many times as is comfortable.

Sexual positions in later life

Advanced sexual positions that rely on stamina, suppleness and an ability to bounce if you fall are not a good idea in later life. Forget swinging from the chandeliers, but at the same time don't resign yourself to using just the missionary position and nothing else. As pleasant as the missionary may be, 50 years of this alone can leave anyone feeling jaded.

Woman-on-top

Women-on-top positions often prove more satisfying for both of you – as well as giving the woman more control, it allows the male to lie back and take things more easily than usual – this is especially helpful if the male has limited mobility or strength due to illness. These positions are also good if he is particularly tired. It is a good idea to use a lubricating gel (water-based if using latex condoms) to cushion the clitoris and penis from prolonged rubbing.

The following woman-on-top positions are popular:

With your partner lying on his back and you lying on top, gently guide his penis into you. Bring your legs inside his for a snug fit. By keeping your legs tightly closed, you can increase the friction between his penis and your vagina and clitoris.

With your partner lying on his back, sit on top of him and lean back, balancing yourself by resting both hands on his knees or thighs. Your partner can then reach forward to caress and massage your breasts, or gently stimulate your clitoris as you move up and down.

With the man kneeling on the bed, the woman sits astride his thighs and gently lowers herself on to his erect penis. She then controls the rate of movement and the depth of penetration. The male also has the freedom to move up and down at the knees and to thrust his pelvis forwards if he wishes. This position is good when the male has a less firm erection, as it allows the penis to stimulate the woman's clitoris and outer vaginal lips, even when not fully hard. However, it might be better avoided if either partner has hip or knee problems.

These positions – like other woman-on-top poses – are excellent for improving clitoral stimulation. They allow the woman to rub forwards and backwards against his pubic bone – as well as lifting up and down on his penis – at varying speeds and depth of penetration. For a more advanced technique, she can introduce a third, twisting, circular movement into the up and down, forwards and backwards motion. By setting her own pace, she can reach orgasm more easily as well as having the freedom to arch her back and extend her neck while feeling fully in control.

At the same time, these positions allow the man full access to his partner's breasts and, as she moves up and down, forwards and backwards, he can also gently stimulate her clitoris with a well-lubricated finger. If he feels he is steaming ahead of her at any time, all he has to do is hold her hips firmly as a pre-arranged signal to stop and rest for a few moments. If he feels energetic, he can also move his pelvis to make gentle thrusting movements, but this position is equally good if the man is particularly tired and his partner is happy to make all the effort while he lies back, relaxes, and watches how his partner responds as she becomes fully aroused. Once your partner is approaching orgasm, you can work together to achieve a simultaneous orgasm, or you can wait for them to come first before climaxing yourself.

Man-on-top

Man-on-top positions allow the male to control the speed and depth of thrusting and to delay his orgasm for a more satisfying experience. The following alternatives to the missionary position are popular.

For better control and deeper penetration, try the following. The woman lies on her back, her buttocks raised on a pillow, and bends one knee up to her chest. Her partner supports his weight with one hand on the bed to the side of her and places his other hand on her bent knee, pushing it down. This lets him thrust deeper and increases the sensation of tightness. However, this position should be avoided if the woman has hip or back problems.

For even deeper, tighter penetration, the woman can lie on her back with her partner on top, then she can bend both knees bringing them in to her chest. Keeping her knees together, she then rests one ankle on each of her partner's shoulders. This lets him push forward, penetrating her as deeply as possible. Her buttocks can be raised higher by resting on a pillow. Again, this position should be avoided if she has hip or back problems.

For the tightest grip on the penis, the woman lies down overhanging the edge of the bed. Her partner kneels down between her legs and pushes forward to enter her. She then reaches down with one hand and makes a V with her fingers, so that a finger slips down on either side of his penis at the base. She squeezes her fingers together to grip her partner firmly as he moves in and out. This position also lets her stimulate her clitoris with her own hand if she wishes, and gives him access to stimulate her breasts and clitoris too.

From behind

Vaginal penetration from behind often gives a woman a more satisfying orgasm as it intensifies the sensation of penetration. The woman leans forward, either supporting herself on the side of the bed, or with her arms back holding her partner's waist. He grasps her waist or buttocks in order to penetrate her more deeply from behind. Alternatively, try kneeling on a bed rather than standing. These positions allow full stroke movement and deep penetration, at the same time as giving the man access to his partner's clitoris and breasts. Another position for vaginal penetration from behind is to make love when lying curled up, side by side, with his front to her back, like spoons.

Oral sex

Many couples enjoy oral sex as part of a loving relationship. There are two types of oral sex: licking and sucking the penis (fellatio) or licking and sucking the clitoris (cunnilingus). Many couples like to shower or bathe together before indulging in oral sex so they can cleanse each other as an erotic part of foreplay. Oral sex can be enjoyable and sexually arousing for both partners, but some people don't fancy it and find the idea distasteful. That is absolutely fine – no one should ever feel pressurised into doing something they don't want to do. Most older people in a long term relationship will already have worked out whether or not oral sex is for them. If you are embarking on a new relationship in later life remember that, like penetrative sex, oral sex also needs to be 'safe' to protect against sexually transmissible infections.

Safer oral sex involves using a barrier. For the man, this means wearing a condom (try flavoured ones). For the woman, this means placing a dental dam – a large, thin square of latex – over her genitals and licking and stimulating her through this.

Soixante-neuf

The so-called position sixty-nine involves you lying on your back (or side) and your partner lying on top (or to one side), head to tail, so that you both have access to each others genitals for simultaneous stimulation. Not everyone likes this position as it can be difficult to concentrate on receiving pleasure while trying to give it at the same time.

Other aids to arousal

Fantasy

The power of imagination and fantasy plays an important role in enhancing and enriching your sex life. Nine out of ten adults regularly use erotic thoughts for sexual arousal, and psychologists have identified four main types of fantasy:

- Those involving past, present or imaginary lovers.
- Scenes indicating sexual power and irresistibility.
- Scenes depicting different settings, practices or positions.
- Scenes focusing on submission or dominance.

You are more likely to fantasise about someone you know than about a famous personality, and around one in three people fantasise about the person they're with at the time.

Some couples find that sharing their fantasies, or acting them out, can be very erotic. Others prefer to keep their intimate images secret. If your relationship is strong, try taking it in turns to share a fantasy as a way of keeping each other's interest alive.

Role playing

Acting out fantasy roles can be fun and exciting. Commonly used themes include:

- strip-tease;
- doctor and nurse;
- nurse and patient;
- naughty French maid;
- naughty boy needing a spanking;
- being tied to the bed;
- dressing up in rubber, leather, silks or chain mail.

Using a mirror

Wherever you make love, using a large mirror can increase your excitement. This adds a voyeuristic element letting you watch each other's facial responses and see your partner's body from different angles.

Vibrators

Vibrators have traditionally been rather tasteless items with a deliberately phallic design. However, this is changing and manufacturers are looking at new ranges of vibrators – now beginning to be referred to as vibes – which are specifically designed to appeal to women. One such range, which has been designed for women by women, has been endorsed by Relate – the couples counselling charity. According to psychosexual therapist Julia Cole, who helped to develop this range, 'Most vibrators are large, penile shapes, which is based on a misunderstanding about a woman's anatomy and where the sensitive areas that need stimulation are found. The female arousal platform is not deep inside but external and just at the entrance to the vagina. Eighty per cent of women fail to reach climax through penetration alone.'

Julia came up with a number of shapes that she drew on paper and then had modelled in wax until she arrived at designs she thought would work. These were tried by over 100 different women who made suggestions for improvement. After some adjustment, prototypes of the range were sent to Relate for comments from their psychosexual therapists. More adjustments were made and it was three years before the products were ready to launch.

Design was not the only disadvantage of the old-fashioned vibrator. Many of those available in the UK were imported and the methods and materials used in production were not necessarily as good as they should be. If you are buying a modern vibrator, it is important to check where it was made and to check that the material it is made from is safe, non-toxic and (preferably) contains Microban to prevent the proliferation of bacteria.

More importantly, traditional vibrators only vibrate at a speed of 40 to 60 Hertz and, as they contain replaceable batteries the speed gets slower and slower as the batteries run down. Yet, research shows that women prefer a speed of 80 Hertz to achieve optimal arousal. Some of the new, female-friendly vibrators are therefore designed to vibrate at 80 Hertz, and are rechargeable so they don't slow down. They are also smaller and lighter to use, as well as quieter, than the previous generation of vibrators.

A vibrator can be used either on your own, or with your partner, to stimulate the penis, testicles and perineum as well as secondary erogenous zones such as the inner thighs, buttocks, behind the knees, soles of the feet or back of the neck. Some people find the vibrations are too intense to use on the tip of the penis or clitoris, but can be pleasant used against the shaft of the penis, or against the side of the clitoris. When used near the clitoris, a vibrator can help many women reach orgasm – sometimes for the first time. The intensity of the stimulation they provide can overcome any psychological blocks preventing orgasm.

3 Changing Body, Changing Needs

The changes wrought by ageing involve a number of unknown challenges that can be very stressful. Change causes uncertainty, uncertainty leads to anxiety and anxiety is a powerful trigger for stress. Have a look at the following list and tick all those that apply to your life now:

- changes in your relationship with your partner;
- changes due to losing your partner;
- changes in your relationships with relatives;
- changes in your social life;
- changes in the type of work you do;
- changes in your living accommodation;
- changes in your health;
- changes in your hobbies/recreations;
- changes in your hours of work – perhaps from full to part-time or retirement.

As well as changes in your lifestyle, changes will be occurring in your body, too. Although you still feel the same inside, the face that looks back at you from the mirror may seem unrecognisable at times, your hair is changing colour (assuming you let it!) and may be noticeably thinner or more sparse than just a few years ago. Your body may also be 'feeling its age', with aches and pains, stiffness and general slowing down.

Bodily changes in men

For men, age-related changes may seem less dramatic than for women as they do not have a cut off point when sex hormone levels suddenly fall. Having said that, some researchers strongly believe in a male form of menopause, that is comparable to the one with which women are familiar.

Male menopause

Testosterone is the main hormone that controls libido in both men and women (see Chapter 2). In older males, testosterone hormone is also responsible for:

- maintenance of sex drive;
- maintenance of the size and function of the penis, testes, prostate gland and scrotum;
- maintenance of erectile function;
- production of sperm so men can remain fertile into their 70s, 80s and even beyond;
- maintenance of male patterns of hair growth, body fat distribution and muscle bulk;
- maintaining the attractiveness of male pheromones (odourless chemicals that play a role in human interactions) to women.

In males, 95 per cent of testosterone hormone is produced by the testicles, with a small amount – around 5 per cent – made elsewhere such as in the adrenal glands. Levels are at their highest during the teens and early twenties, and gradually reduce in later life. Testosterone secretion also varies with the time of day, and is highest in the morning, falling by 20–30 per cent by the end of the day. Small amounts of testosterone are naturally converted to the so-called 'female hormone' oestrogen in body fat stores – an effect that is more pronounced in overweight males.

Although circulating levels of testosterone naturally fall slightly during middle age, this effect is usually small at less than 1 per cent a year – beginning around the age of 40 – and usually goes unnoticed. Unlike the female menopause, men do not experience a sudden drop in hormones but some males do develop abnormally low levels of testosterone. Research suggests this affects around 7 per cent of men aged 40–60 years, 20 per cent of men aged 60–80 years, and around 35 per cent of men aged over 80 years. These more pronounced falls in testosterone levels result from underactive testicles – a medical condition known as hypogonadism. These low levels of testosterone are linked with symptoms of tiredness, irritability, lowered sex drive, aching joints, dry skin, insomnia, excessive sweating, hot flushes and depression. Because these symptoms are so similar to those experienced by menopausal women, they are often referred to as the male menopause or andropause.

There are also some males who experience symptoms of andropause despite having normal circulating levels of testosterone hormone. Most testosterone circulates in the bloodstream where it is bound to proteins. This binding reduces its overall effects. It is only the remaining free testosterone (around 2 per cent of the total) that remains active. When symptoms – including sexual difficulties – occur in older males despite a normal testosterone level, this may be due to more testosterone becoming bound to protein (and therefore less active) in the circulation, or to cells losing their ability to detect the normal level of active testosterone that is present.

Hormone replacement therapy for men

Male hormone replacement therapy with testosterone is available to treat low sex drive when associated with clinically confirmed low levels of free (unbound) testosterone. Treatment aims to raise testosterone levels to normal, not to excessively high levels, and will not produce an excessive sex drive. When given to men with normal testosterone levels, it has little significant effect on sex drive and performance. It can, however, restore libido to its previous level for those experiencing problems due to low testosterone activity.

A few doctors are prepared to prescribe testosterone therapy to middle-aged and older men with low sex drive – even where the testicles are not functioning below par – because they are convinced their body cells cannot interact with testosterone as well as in their youth. Other doctors disagree, and place more emphasis on improving general lifestyle factors (stress, smoking, alcohol intake) instead.

Testosterone replacement therapy is only available on prescription, usually from specialist clinics. It is not suitable for all males and can cause a number of side effects which your doctor will tell you about if he or she feels you might benefit from treatment. A synthetic androgen, mesterolone, is also available as a tablet for treating androgen deficiency and male infertility.

Non-hormonal ways of helping the male menopause include:

- stopping smoking;
- drinking less alcohol;
- taking a multi-nutrient supplement as deficiencies of vitamins and minerals can exacerbate hormonal imbalances;
- taking more exercise;
- checking that symptoms aren't due to prescribed medications;
- seeking counselling for relationship or sexual difficulties.

Prostate problems

Many men know more about a woman's monthly cycle than they do about their own body and its sexual health, yet problems with the prostate gland are as common in older males as period problems in younger women. Because the gland is hidden away deep in the plumbing, and because it generally behaves itself until middle age, it comes as something of a shock when it starts to go wrong.

The prostate is a sexual and reproductive gland that is only found in males. It lies just below the base of the bladder and is wrapped around the urethra – the tube through which urine flows from the bladder to the outside world.

Before the age of around 40 years, the healthy prostate gland is similar in size and shape to a large chestnut. From around the age of 45, however, the number of cells in the prostate gland increases and the gland starts to enlarge in most men. This is a non-cancerous process known as benign prostatic hyperplasia or BPH for short.

Problems resulting from an enlarged prostate

BPH is a normal process and, in the early stages, is not classed as a disease. It is only when growth becomes greater than required and starts to affect urinary flow that symptoms start to arise. In some men, the prostate gland grows large without causing problems with passing water. In many men, however, enlargement of the prostate gland squeezes the urethra to interfere with urinary flow. Spasm of the stretched smooth muscle fibres within the gland also contribute to squeezing of the urethra and the development of a number of embarrassing urinary symptoms which doctors refer to as prostatism. These include:

- straining or difficulty when starting to pass water;
- a weak urinary stream which may start and stop mid-flow;
- dribbling of urine after voiding;
- having to rush to the toilet;
- passing water more often than normal;
- having to get up to pass urine at night;
- discomfort when passing water;
- a feeling of not having emptied the bladder fully;
- urinary incontinence;
- urinary retention.

NB Blood in the urine or sperm is not a usual symptom of BPH. If you notice this, you must see your doctor as soon as possible as this needs further investigation.

The need to pass water at night disturbs the sleep of both the sufferer and his bed partner, which can lead to friction in a relationship. This will be even more likely if sexual activity is also affected due to erectile dysfunction (see below).

BPH is one of the most common medical conditions to affect men over the age of 50, and the single most common problem dealt with by urologists. One study of over 700 men suggested that symptoms affect

14 per cent of men aged 40–49 and 50 per cent of men aged 60–69. Overall, it produced symptoms in 25 per cent of men aged 40–79. By the age of 80, it is estimated that as many as 80 per cent of men are affected. It has been estimated that a man aged 40 years has a 1 in 3 chance of undergoing a surgical operation for prostate enlargement during later life.

The exact cause of BPH remains unknown, but most researchers agree that enlargement of the prostate gland is linked with testosterone and its breakdown products. One theory is that it may be linked to the relative lowering of testosterone levels and corresponding increase in oestrogen levels that occur with age. In this changing hormone environment, the response of the prostate gland seems to be to grow so that it can absorb a greater proportion of the available testosterone.

Once in the prostate cells, testosterone is converted into another, more powerful male hormone, dihydrotestosterone (DHT). This conversion is controlled by a prostate enzyme, 5-alpha reductase. It is DHT that is responsible for triggering division of prostate cells so their numbers increase. Levels of DHT are known to be five times higher in enlarged prostate glands than in those of normal size. If the conversion of testosterone to DHT is prevented, BPH does not occur and can even be reversed once it has developed.

BPH and your love life

The symptoms of BPH can have a drastic effect on a man's life. They can lead to depression, low self-esteem, social isolation and even being confined to home due to the difficulty of having to find public toilets at short notice.

In a study of over 400 men aged 40–79 with BPH, researchers found that 51 per cent reported symptoms that interfered with at least one of a number of selected daily activities such as drinking fluids before travel or bedtime, sleeping, or driving for two hours without a break. The symptoms also limited their going to places without toilets, playing outdoor sports or visiting the cinema, theatre or church. For 17 per cent of these men, the interference occurred most or all of the time.

Another survey of 800 men over the age of 50 found that almost half of sexually active males with symptoms due to an enlarged prostate gland experienced a lower sex drive, problems maintaining an erection, and problems with ejaculation. As a result, half as many men with prostate symptoms made love at least once a week compared with those without problems (20 per cent versus 40 per cent).

Further research involving 168 men with BPH found that 59 per cent had a low sex drive, 56 per cent had infrequent erections with 46 per cent fulfilling criteria for impotence, and 38 per cent had ejaculation problems.

This was confirmed in a larger study of 423 men with BPH in the community and 1271 men attending urology clinics which also found that sexual problems were common. Rigidity of erections was reduced in 60 per cent of men with BPH (versus 53 per cent in the community), reduced ejaculation in 62 per cent (versus 47 per cent) and pain on ejaculation in 17 per cent (versus 5 per cent). Sex lives were admitted as spoiled by lower urinary tract symptoms in 8 per cent of men in the community and 46 per cent of those in the clinic.

It is clear that many men with prostate symptoms also have sexual problems, and it is important that couples affected do not suffer in silence but seek help.

If you suspect you have symptoms of prostatism, it is important to tell your doctor as soon as possible. Don't wait until symptoms become troublesome and start interfering with your life. Early screening will help to prevent complications. It also means that the more serious but potentially curable problem of prostate cancer – which can produce similar initial symptoms – is picked up early and treated sooner rather than later.

In most cases where lifestyle is severely disrupted, your doctor should be happy to either refer you to a urology specialist, or to prescribe a drug treatment. Drugs are available that can help reduce spasm of the prostate gland, or help shrink it down. If your doctor decides that treatment is not yet necessary, or will not suit you, another option is to take the herbal remedy saw palmetto.

Over 20 randomised, double-blind, placebo-controlled trials have shown that standardised extracts of saw palmetto berries are effective in relieving mild to moderate symptoms of BPH. One of the best ways of evaluating the mixed results of a number of studies is a meta-analysis. This is a study which pools data from comparable trials to give an average of the results from as many patients as possible. This method was applied to studies involving saw palmetto and published in the Journal of the American Medical Association. A total of 18 studies involving 2939 men found that, compared with men receiving inactive placebo, saw palmetto fruit extracts improved urinary tract symptoms by 28 per cent, night time frequency by 25 per cent, urinary flow by 28 per cent and reduced the amount of urine remaining in the bladder after voiding by 43 per cent. No significant side effects were reported. In trials where saw palmetto extracts were compared with a variety of drugs prescribed to improve prostate symptoms, the herbal extracts were found to be at least as effective – but with fewer unwanted side effects such as erectile dysfunction. If you have symptoms of prostate problems, do see your doctor for full assessment before deciding whether or not to take saw palmetto fruit extracts, however. These extracts should ideally only be used once you have had prostate cancer ruled out.

Prostate cancer and sexuality

Prostate cancer can cause problems with erections in a number of ways. As the tumour most commonly develops in the outer part of the gland, it may not produce symptoms when passing water until the condition is fairly advanced. Before these symptoms appear, however, the tumour may affect the nerve bundles that help to control erection, or affect structures known as the seminal vesicles that normally produce male fluids essential for normal ejaculation and orgasm. The drugs, surgical procedures and radiotherapy regimes that may be used to treat prostate cancer will also affect sexuality. Prostate – and other – cancers can also lead to weakness, anaemia, loss of well-being and the gradual onset of pain which can, not surprisingly, also affect sexual activity. On top of that, anxiety, fear and depression can reduce sex drive and lead to relationship difficulties at a time when close companionship is vital to maintain a positive outlook on life.

Some men with prostate cancer may be advised to have their testicles inactivated, to drastically reduce levels of testosterone hormone. The effects on your sex life need to be carefully considered, as nine out of ten men who have their testicles inactivated through drug treatment (or surgical removal) will develop a complete loss of sex drive, and total inability to achieve erections. Another effect of treatment is the loss of muscle bulk and the development of a more feminine redistribution of body fat which can have profound effects on self-esteem. At least one in four men with prostate cancer will already have experienced a con- siderable restriction in their sex life as a result of their condition, however, and those who are not sexually active may not find this unduly worrying.

If the prostate gland is surgically removed (radical prostatectomy), 98 per cent of males are likely to experience difficulty in getting or main- taining erections unless the surgeon uses careful techniques to spare the nerves controlling erection. When these techniques are used, erec- tile difficulties after the operation can be avoided in over 60 per cent of males. Radical prostatectomy can also change the experience of orgasm by removing the valve that stops semen passing back into the bladder at orgasm. As a result, a male may ejaculate backwards rather than forwards (retrograde ejaculation) so the orgasm is 'dry'. Some men find this a problem, others don't. It is not harmful in any way, as sperm are passed along with urine next time the bladder is emptied. The condition does cause infertility however, and medical assistance is needed if the affected male wishes to father a child.

Radiotherapy to treat prostate cancer can also cause sexual problems with reduced libido during treatment, difficulty in getting or maintaining erections in 50 per cent of men (25 per cent with a procedure known as brachytherapy). It is also common to notice a reduced production of semen after radiotherapy, and there may be difficulty achieving orgasm. Radiotherapy will also affect a man's ability to father a child, and some men – particularly those who have younger partners – may wish to consider banking sperm before treatment.

Hormonal treatment of prostate cancer is also likely to cause sexual problems. It is obviously very important to discuss the possible effects of treatment on your future sex life. Ideally, this topic will be raised by your oncologist when talking about treatment choices and potential side effects. If he or she doesn't raise the topic, don't feel embarrassed about asking yourself.

Although this may sound very gloomy, there is hope. For those who are sexually active, newer forms of treatment for prostate cancer, known as androgen receptor therapy, have been developed which maintain a normal or even slightly elevated serum testosterone level. As a result, three quarters of men who are suitable for this form of treatment can maintain a reasonable libido and level of sexual activity. Up to one in three may develop painful enlargement of breast tissue (gynaecomastia) however, which can in itself affect enjoyment of sexual activity. For other men, erections can sometimes be restored through drugs such as Viagra (see page 118) and many men are able to recover the ability to ejaculate small amounts of fluid and to enjoy orgasm.

Bodily changes in women

The stereotype of the ageing, grey-haired 'little, old lady' is now passé – glamorous older females such as Joan Collins are wonderful icons for women who prefer to age gracefully and slowly. Although hormone replacement therapy is not the panacea it was once believed to be, cosmetic surgery and advances in cosmetics (as well as better general health) mean it can be increasingly difficult to guess a woman's age.

Female menopause

After the menopause, a woman's body slowly changes in a number of ways that can understandably affect her self confidence and sexuality:

- oestrogen withdrawal leads to a reduction in breast size compared to other parts of the body (unless you are generally gaining weight);
- loss of pubic hair can occur along with lowered libido, reduced muscle mass and lowered energy levels;
- changes in body weight and body shape may widen the gap between social ideals of beauty and the image a woman sees in the mirror;
- skin ageing, thinning hair and increased appearance of wrinkles and age spots can further affect a woman's sexual identity.

Lack of oestrogen also affects emotions as, although not many people realise it, the brain contains oestrogen receptors too. All these changes can be difficult to adapt to and symptoms seem to be worse if you have been under prolonged stress. Usually, up to 5 per cent of circulating female sex hormones are made by the adrenal glands. As the ovaries stop working at the menopause, the adrenal glands take over some of their function and produce small amounts of oestrogen, as well as doubling their output of testosterone. If a woman has been under long-term stress, however, her adrenal glands may already be working flat out producing stress hormones such as adrenaline. As a result, when the menopause approaches, there are no extra reserves to help boost the output of adrenal sex hormones. Stressed women therefore tend to suffer more and worse menopausal symptoms (eg hot flushes, night sweats) than women who have fewer pressures and less adverse stress to contend with in their life. They are also more likely to suffer a reduction in their sex drive.

Hot flushes are experienced by around 80 per cent of women. They can, in themselves, have a profound effect on a woman's sexuality and how attractive she feels. It is difficult to believe you are sexy when you are hot, sticky, uncomfortable, and can feel your face flaming red. The tendency towards hot flushes usually only lasts one or two years as it coincides with a larger than usual fluctuation in hormone levels. Each hot flush usually lasts between one and five minutes, although occasionally one may last an hour or more. Some women suffer up to 12 hot flushes a day, while others may only get one in an entire week. The flush is usually felt over the upper trunk, neck, face and arms. Blood vessels in the skin dilate to increase blood flow so that the skin becomes red and hot. Skin temperature rises by 1 to 4 degrees Celsius – enough to make any woman feel sweaty and uncomfortable, even though her internal body temperature stays much the same.

Women who suffer from hot flushes seem to be more sensitive to lowered oestrogen levels than women who do not flush. As a result, they tend to develop more – and more unpleasant – menopausal symptoms than those who do not flush.

Help for menopausal problems

Keeping cool through a hot flush

If you develop a flush, don't be embarrassed. Breath in deeply, sit still and try to relax. The following tips may also be helpful:

- concentrate on breathing deeply and slowly;
- cool down with a chilled drink, sucking an ice-cube or eating ice cream;
- try to sit down near an open window or door so you can breathe fresh, cool air;
- carry a small, battery-operated personal fan in your bag for emergencies;
- carry a small packet of wet wipes to help you freshen up until you can wash or change;
- carry a small wash bag around with you containing flannel, soap, towel and deodorant;
- you may also need a larger bag for a crease-proof change of clothes.

Dealing with night sweats

Night sweats can also affect sexuality. You may wake drenched and with an unpleasant sensation of difficulty breathing, or you may wake feeling cold and clammy. You may be so soaked in sweat that you need to change your nightie and bed linen. Once sweat evaporates you will often feel clammy and chilled, so feelings of hot and cold may alternate.

If you wake at night with a sweat or flush, you may be able to freshen up and go straight back to sleep. Many women find it difficult to get back to sleep, and end up tossing and turning. So sleep is difficult and making love is the last thing on their mind.

If you suffer from night sweats, keep a fan by the side of your bed to help cool you down. A bottle of chilled mineral water (eg kept in a wine cooler) will also help you to freshen up as you sip it slowly. Other suggestions that may help include:

- try using sheets and layers of blankets rather than a duvet, so you can quickly adjust the amount of covers on your side of the bed;
- keep spare sheets easily to hand for a quick change when the bed is drenched – there's nothing worse than trying to get back to sleep in a wet bed;
- you may find it is easier to sleep with several single sheets and two duvets on a double bed so you disturb your sleeping partner less.

Hormone replacement therapy (HRT)

Some women find hormone replacement therapy helpful, although it is not suitable for everyone and more natural alternatives are preferable for some. See Chapter 5 for more information on HRT.

Black cohosh

There is good evidence that extracts derived from the herb, black cohosh, can help reduce hot flushes, night sweats, feelings of depression, anxiety, tension and mood swings. It seems to have a direct action on centres of the brain that help to control dilation of blood vessels.

Black cohosh is the most widely used and thoroughly studied natural alternative to hormone replacement therapy (HRT). Several comparison studies have shown standardised extracts of black cohosh to produce better results in relieving hot flushes, thinning of the vaginal tissues and associated dryness, as well as depression and anxiety compared to standard HRT (conjugated oestrogens). Trials suggest that four out of five women taking it describe its effects as either good or very good.

A German trial has shown that black cohosh plus St John's wort was effective in treating 78 per cent of women with hot flushes and other menopausal problems. Most women experience significant improvement in symptoms within two to four weeks. In another study, black cohosh out performed diazepam and oestrogen HRT in relieving depressive moods and anxiety. It will not protect against coronary heart disease or osteoporosis however.

Because its unique oestrogen action does not stimulate oestrogen-sensitive tumours (and may even inhibit them) black cohosh extracts have been used in women with a history of breast cancer, although this should only be done under the supervision of a qualified medical herbalist.

As black cohosh has a positive effect on female sex hormones, it may be used to improve low sex drive associated with the menopause.

Isoflavones

Isoflavones are oestrogen-like plant hormones found mainly in members of the pea and bean family such as soya and chickpeas. Isoflavones have an oestrogen-like action in the body which is five hundred to one thousand times weaker than that of human oestrogens. These plant hormones can therefore provide a useful additional hormone boost when oestrogen levels are low after the menopause.

In cultures such as Japan where soy is a dietary staple, intakes of isoflavones are 50–100mg per day compared with a typical western consumption of only 2–5mg per day. Blood levels of phytoestrogens in Japan are therefore as much as 110 times higher than those typically found in western women. As a result, less than 25 per cent of menopausal Japanese women complain of hot flushes, compared with 85 per cent of North American women.

In one study involving over a hundred post-menopausal women, isoflavones from soya extracts significantly reduced the number of hot flushes experienced per day. By the 12th week of treatment, women taking soy had a 45 per cent reduction in hot flushes versus only 30 per cent with placebo.

Isoflavones mimic some of the beneficial effects of oestrogen on the circulation, helping to dilate coronary arteries, increase heart function, reduce blood levels of harmful LDL-cholesterol (typically by 10 per cent) and reduce blood stickiness to prevent unwanted clotting. These findings may help to explain why the Japanese have one of the lowest rates of coronary heart disease in the world.

Based on evidence from over 50 independent studies, the US Food and Drug Administration (FDA) has authorised health claims on food labels that 'A diet low in saturated fat and cholesterol, and which includes 25g soya protein per day, can significantly reduce the risk of coronary heart disease'.

Phytoestrogens also have a beneficial action on bone, boosting formation of new bone and reducing absorption of old bone. A good intake of isoflavones has been shown to significantly increase bone mineral content and density in the lumber spine and to protect against spinal bone loss and osteoporosis.

Breast cancer

One in nine women will eventually develop breast cancer in the UK. The good news is that earlier diagnosis and better treatments mean the long-term outlook for those developing the disease is often excellent. One aspect of breast cancer that may be ignored is the effect it will have on your sex life, however. When you are first diagnosed with breast cancer, your mental strength and treatment is focused on survival. Once you are through this period and are well on the road to recovery, you may be faced with issues that affect your sexuality and sense of femininity. Many women with breast cancer will have been used to a healthy and active sex life before their illness was diagnosed. Afterwards, as a result of treatment such as surgery (either lumpectomy or mastectomy) and radiotherapy they may find their physical shape is changed, and may feel lacking in energy as a result of chemotherapy or hormone treatment. Researchers have found that under 10 per cent of women experience sexual problems following a lumpectomy, but that this rises to around 35 per cent of women undergoing radical mastectomy. Most sexual problems involve difficulty in adjusting to a new body image as coping with both physical and mental scarring makes many women understandably reluctant to share intimacy with their partner – at a time when they really need to feel close to someone. Treatment for breast cancer also seems to have a significant adverse effect on sexuality, with research suggesting that, although 80 per cent of women with advanced breast cancer considered sex was an important part of their life, only 25 per cent found it easy to experience sexual pleasure after their diagnosis. This can be related either to the treatment (in particular the content of some of the drugs used to combat breast cancer) or to the feelings about body image and femininity that such a diagnosis can provoke. Often, both factors will have some influence.

The partners of women with breast cancer will also be facing their own anxieties and may be concerned about making sexual demands in case she doesn't feel ready, or well enough. They may also fear that touching their partner may cause her physical pain.

It is important to tell your doctor if you are experiencing sexual problems. Ideally, this topic will be raised by your oncologist when talking about treatment choices and potential side effects. If he or she doesn't raise the topic – don't feel embarrassed about asking yourself. Researchers have found that women who seek information about the effects of treatment on their sex life adjust significantly better to treatment than those who don't.

Even though you have had breast cancer, your doctor may still be happy to prescribe certain forms of oestrogen replacement therapy to overcome sexual problems such as vaginal dryness. See Chapter 5 for more detailed information.

The effects of long-term illnesses on sexuality in later life

Many long-term diseases such as those affecting the heart, circulation, kidneys, liver, reproductive, urinary and nervous systems are accompanied by loss of sex drive. In some cases this is due to metabolic changes in body salts, with extreme tiredness, or with physical disabilities that may cause pain, embarrassment or feelings of sexual unattractiveness. In some cases, the treatment of the disease itself (eg certain cancers) may have a profound effect on hormone balance, anatomy or sexuality. Many other people with the same illness as yourself will have experienced the same problems. It is therefore worth contacting any relevant self-help groups dedicated to your particular type of illness to see if they can help. Often, patient self-help groups have written booklets on sexual problems or can offer advice on ways to overcome them (see Useful Addresses, page 167 onwards).

Most long-term illnesses will affect your sexuality on a number of levels. Some illnesses, such as multiple sclerosis, can affect the nerves involved in sexual sensations and response, so there is lowered libido, altered genital sensation (eg, numbness, pain, burning, or discomfort), reduced lubrication and changes in the ability to reach orgasm and in its intensity.

The illness itself may produce physical changes which affect sexual response indirectly, such as fatigue, weakness, muscle spasms, pain, problems with mobility and changes to bladder or bowel control, as well as the side effects of medication.

Sexual problems can also result from the emotional effects of a long-term illness, such as negative self-image, poor self-esteem, anxiety, depression, mood swings, a sense of having lost one's femininity/masculinity as well as anger and feelings of 'why me?'. You will also be worried about the effects of your illness on your partner, and have unspoken anxieties about being abandoned, being a burden, or not being able to satisfy your loved one sexually any more.

Serious illness either in yourself or those you are close to is a powerful cause of stress, especially when there is uncertainty – over the diagnosis, the best treatment or whether a full recovery is possible. Some illnesses and accidents have temporary effects from which you can expect to make a full recovery. This allows you to achieve a sense of closure on the episode so you can carry on with life much as before. When an illness or injury has long-term consequences, however, your life will inevitably change from the way it used to be. Major illness or injury can be very stressful and produce a number of changes in your physical and emotional health. These may include:

- worrying about the significance of various symptoms;
- having to endure a series of tests;
- waiting for results;
- having to face a serious diagnosis;
- feeling numb;
- coping with pain;
- coping with immobility;
- coping with changes in certain bodily functions;
- coping with treatments that may have unpleasant side effects;
- having to face surgery;
- fear of disfigurement;
- frustration at infirmity;
- anger – feelings of 'Why me?' or 'Why us?'
- guilt or remorse – feelings of 'if only';
- uncertainty and fear about the future;
- changes in family income or outgoings – illness can be expensive;
- worry about how loved ones will cope;

■ fear that things are being kept from you;

■ fear of loss of control;

■ coming to terms with your own mortality.

It is no good dwelling on what might have been or what you could have done differently. The best way to fight any illness is to face it head on, steel yourself for what lies ahead and make plans about the best way to cope. Negative thinking will drag you down and slow the healing process. If you are feeling stressed by illness or pain, it can help to practise a breathing exercise, a relaxation technique or to visualise yourself fighting the illness and becoming well again.

After a traumatic event like a major illness, it is common to suffer from post-traumatic stress disorder in which you may experience anxiety, flashbacks, panic attacks and difficulty sleeping as well as depression and feelings of guilt, remorse, anger or even shame. Don't bottle your emotions up – let them out. Talk about your feelings and once you have made a good recovery, try to get back to normal as soon as possible within the limits of your condition. If you feel you need extra help however, don't be afraid to ask for it. If necessary, your doctor can refer you for counselling – which is especially important if you are suffering the effects of post-traumatic stress.

Counselling after illness, or before treatment

Different people have different expectations of illnesses and their treatment in later life. Ideally, doctors caring for people with different health problems should consider how your particular health condition or its treatment will affect your sexual desires and activities. Where sexual problems are highly likely as a result of illness, medication or surgery, this should be discussed before treatment is started, rather than after when the effects have already occurred. If your doctor doesn't bring up the topic, don't be embarrassed to mention it yourself – all doctors are used to answering people's questions about sex. The following checklist will help to ensure important areas are covered with you and your partner:

- What would you consider an acceptable level of sexual function?
- What are the risks of erectile problems associated with different treatment options?
- What are the possible effects of different treatments on:
  - production of ejaculatory fluids?
  - achieving orgasm?
  - quality of orgasm?
- What are the risks of ejaculating backwards into the bladder, rather than forwards as normal (retrograde ejaculation)?
- What are the effects on fertility (where an older male may still wish to father children)?
- Are sperm bank facilities available for use before treatment if desired?
- What is the risk of shortening of the penis following radiation therapy?
- What options are available to treat erectile problems that might result from treatment?
- Can you receive psychosexual counselling or relationship counselling before or after treatment if you wish?

Talking about these fears with your partner, so you share your feelings and concerns, will help you both feel more in control of what is happening and more able to accept future changes.

Heart attack and sexuality

A heart attack is a dramatic event that often comes as a complete shock – especially for those who did not even realise they were at risk. A major event such as this can produce profound changes in the way you think and behave.

People who have experienced a heart attack are understandably anxious about having sex afterwards. Researchers have found that the level of sexual activity often decreases because of the fear it may trigger another heart attack. Problems achieving an erection due to anxiety are also more common after a heart attack than before. In most cases, however, there is no reason why you should not return to a normal and fulfilling sex life once you have recovered from the heart attack and got your life back on track. In fact, resuming sexual activity is an important part of getting your life back to normal. As a form of exercise, sex can be positively beneficial for heart health as it provides the same level of exertion as a brisk 20 minute walk or playing 18 holes of golf, with some experts declaring orgasm as the equivalent to walking up two flights of stairs.

The fear of sexual activity triggering a fatal heart attack is considerable, but the actual risk seems to be small – assuming you are with your usual partner. Whether or not someone has heart disease, the biggest risk of a heart attack occurring is in the two hours following sex. For those with a healthy heart, research suggests the risk is as small as two in a million. If someone has coronary disease the risk rises tenfold, but is still only 20 in a million, or 1 in 50,000. That risk is still quite small, so those who are afraid to have sex after a heart attack should find this reassuring. For those who exercise regularly, and who are relatively fit, the risk is even lower. The researchers based these findings on interviews with over 1,600 men and women who had had a heart attack, but did not ask what kind of sex they had, the intensity, or whether or not it was extramarital. Previous research does suggest that the majority of heart attacks occurring in older people during – or immediately after – sexual activity occur during the course of an extra marital affair, possibly due to the heightened level of guilt and excitement.

Do be guided by your doctor, who will know the extent of your heart attack and how much exercise you can reasonably expect to enjoy without harm. Most doctors agree that, as long as you do not experience symptoms such as breathlessness or chest pain during exertion, then resuming a normal sex life as soon as you feel ready is fine. Wait until at least two weeks after your heart attack, however, and preferably after you have had an exercise stress test to determine how well your heart copes with exercise. If you have two or more major risk factors for heart disease (eg high blood pressure, obesity, diabetes, smoking, high cholesterol, lack of exercise) then it makes sense to wait until eight weeks after your heart attack before attempting sex again.

If you are in any doubt, always ask your doctor. Don't be embarrassed or shy, as every adult – including your doctor – has a right to a fulfilling sex life.

Assuming your doctor has given you the go-ahead, choose a time when you feel rested and relaxed, and are in a familiar setting.

Avoid sex:

- within two hours of eating;
- if you are upset, tired or stressed;
- if are feeling under the weather or unwell;
- if exercise brings on breathlessness or chest pain.

If you do experience chest pain or breathlessness on exertion, then stop immediately and contact your doctor. It is possible that taking medication to control these symptoms (eg sublingual glyceryl trinitrate) may solve the problem.

Your partner may be understandably apprehensive about initiating sex with you – just as you may feel anxious about approaching them. Sexual intimacy can take several forms, however, and even if you don't feel up to full sexual intercourse, it is important to show affection through touching, holding, kissing and caressing so your partner does not feel isolated or pushed away.

Talk about your fears openly with your partner and avoid strenuous positions – usually someone who has had a heart attack is advised to play a passive rather than an active role.

With increasing age, male sexual function can also be affected by a number of other health problems, including:

- diabetes, which can affect ability to achieve erection;
- neurological conditions such as Parkinsonism or multiple sclerosis;
- circulatory diseases such as hardening and furring up of the arteries (atherosclerosis) or raised blood pressure (hypertension);
- side effects of medication, especially treatments for high blood pressure, depression and prostate cancer.

Stroke and sexuality

A stroke is a serious and frightening condition from which most people make a good recovery. Many people make a full recovery although the initial period of adjustment and improvement can take many months. Most people who have had a stroke worry about resuming their sex life, either because they are worried sex might trigger another attack or because the stroke itself has affected sexual desire and function. In both men and women, stroke can reduce libido in around one in two people – sometimes this is due to the part of the brain which was affected by the stroke, but more often it seems to be linked with medication. It can also result from anxiety, depression, impaired self-image and loss of self-esteem. Research suggests that where libido is reduced in males, it often returns within seven weeks although this will vary from person to person. Stroke can also interfere with a man's ability to sustain an erection, experience orgasm or achieve ejaculation. It can also make orgasm more difficult to reach in women and reduce vaginal lubrication. In addition, familiar sexual positions that were once comfortable may now prove difficult or impossible to sustain. Fears about performance can reduce sexual interest and some people develop depression following their stroke. While this is quite normal, and in most cases disappears within three months, it does tend to make any sexual problems worse. The most common worry is that sex will make the stroke recur or exacerbate your condition.

Although this all sounds very negative, people who have had a stroke, and their partners, can be reassured that sexual activity is not a major factor in causing a stroke. The chance that another stroke will occur during lovemaking is extremely low, and it is perfectly acceptable for your heart to beat faster and for you to become slightly breathless when making love. The amount of exertion is around the same as that needed to walk up two flights of stairs. If you were sexually active before your stroke, you can probably be sexually active again given enough time, patience and loving support. After recovery many people find the same forms of lovemaking they enjoyed beforehand are still rewarding and there is no reason why you should not resume your usual sexual activity as soon as you feel ready to do so. If partial paralysis or weakness is the main problem affecting your ability to make love, try experimenting with different positions so you find one you can cope with. You can also use soft cushions or pillows to provide additional support for your affected side. If an arm or leg goes into spasms, this can often be minimised by lying on the affected limb and bending it slightly.

Begin slowly. Choose a time when you feel at your best and not tired at the end of a long day. Some doctors advise having sex before a meal rather than after – it is best to wait three hours after a heavy meal to give yourself time to digest the meal. Perhaps first thing in the morning, after washing and before breakfast, would be a good time to choose.

Start by just being close to your partner, and enjoy touching and caressing each other. When you feel ready, start to explore what feels good and how any changes in sensation in parts of your body feel different. Let your partner know what feels nice, and what feels odd or unpleasant – good communication is the key.

And remember – you don't have to have full penetrative sex until you are ready – caressing, kissing, mutual massage and using tasteful sex toys such as one of the modern vibrators (see page 49) are all perfectly normal and acceptable activities.

If you have a troubling and persistent loss of sexual desire, or an inability to make love, do seek medical advice. Often, changing your medication, or prescribing a drug such as Viagra (see page 118) will significantly improve the situation. Psychosexual counselling to help overcome anxiety surrounding sex is also helpful.

If you don't feel ready for sex, however, you can still show affection to each other through kissing, cuddling and caressing. Even just holding hands will show that you care.

Bladder problems

If difficulties in controlling your bladder are a problem for you, it will be helpful to limit fluid intake for two hours before making love, and empty your bladder before sex. If you have a urinary catheter, ask your doctor if you can remove it for sex, in which case you or your partner will need to learn how it put it back in place afterwards. If it is best not to remove the catheter, this should not interfere too much with making love as far as a woman with a catheter is concerned – it can be taped to your thigh or up over your abdomen with a strip of surgical tape to help ensure it is not accidentally tugged out. Using a water-based lubricant (eg KY jelly) when making love will also help to reduce any friction that might pull the catheter out. For a male who is fitted with a catheter, it can usually be folded back over his erect penis and covered with a pre-lubricated condom into which you have squirted a teaspoon of water-based gel (eg KY Jelly) to reduce friction and irritation between the catheter and penis.

How your changing body can affect your sexuality

Sexuality is not just the act of sexual intercourse – it also involves your emotions, how feminine or masculine you feel, and how attractive you are to both yourself and others. It involves self-esteem, care over how you present yourself, and the ability to enjoy a warm, loving and tactile relationship even where full penetrative sex does not occur.

Changing body, changing perceptions

How you feel about your body and sexuality will have changed whether as a result of just growing older, or of both growing older and having to cope with a long-term illness. How you cope with these changes will affect how you feel about your sexuality. If your body has changed in a significant way, it is normal to feel bereavement for what you have lost and to go through stages of panic, helplessness, denial, depression and even anger. By learning to deal with these feelings, in time you will begin to accept these changes – even though your body may have changed it still belongs to you and you are still the same person inside.

Many people find sex awkward because they are ashamed of some aspect of their body. This can be even more of a problem for someone who has been without a partner for some time and who would like to reactivate this part of their life. The following exercise in total honesty can be helpful for people who are currently in a long term relationship, and for those who are not.

Take off all your clothes in a warm room in front of a full-length mirror. Gentle, relaxing music will help as this exercise takes time to do properly.

Study your face, breasts/chest, shoulders, waist, hips, bottom, thighs and ankles in a critical manner. Turn sideways onto the mirror and study your profile and rear view too. A triple mirror, or another long mirror placed at an angle makes this easier. Don't be afraid to be honest. It's the only way to galvanise yourself into action.

If you only focus on parts of your body that you don't like, you will feel unattractive – whether it's fat thighs, flabby arms, stretch marks or scars from surgery. The best way to deal with imperfections is to balance them with your good points and to work out ways of improving those bits that can be changed. This exercise will help you learn to view yourself as a whole, rather than focusing only on the bits that embarrass you in some way.

Write down a list of as many good points about yourself that you can find, eg:

- my lips are full;
- my hair is thick and healthy;
- my skin is soft and supple;
- my tummy is firm and flat;
- my breasts are normal;
- my legs are nice and long.

Concentrate on these good points and allow yourself to feel good about them.

Now write down a list of all the negative things you thought about your body, eg:

- my lips are too thin;
- my skin is dry;
- my hair needs cutting;
- my breasts are too large (or too small);
- I'm beginning to get a paunch;
- my legs need more muscular definition;
- I have an obvious surgical scar/loss of part of my body.

Many of these negative points may be easily remedied (see below), so don't let them get you down.

Having studied your body, put on some loose, comfortable clothes and think about your personality and emotions. Write down all the positive things you can think of, eg:

- I am easy going;
- I have a good sense of humour;
- I get on well with people;
- I am caring and loyal;
- I am sensitive to other people's feelings;
- I am honest.

Concentrate on these good points and allow yourself to feel good about them.

Finally, write down all the negative thoughts about your personality and emotions that come into your head, eg:

- I get bored easily;
- I feel too tired for exercise;
- I keep putting things off;
- I need constant reassurance;
- I no longer feel sexy;
- Nobody could love me;
- I feel angry at what has happened to me;
- I keep pushing my mate away.

Now look at the lists containing negative physical and emotional statements and turn these round into positive ones including any solutions.

Use the present tense as this helps your mind imprint the positive statements more easily. For example:

- 'My lips look thin' becomes 'Make-up techniques help my lips look thicker'.
- 'My skin is dry' becomes 'Softening my skin with a body lotion and treating myself to a salt scrub and aromatherapy massage helps my skin become supple'.
- 'My hair needs cutting' becomes 'My hair looks great – especially now I visit the hairdresser regularly'.
- 'My breasts are too large' becomes 'My breasts are a perfectly acceptable part of me'.
- 'I'm beginning to develop a paunch' becomes 'My waistline easily becomes more slender due to my new healthy diet and exercise plan'.
- 'My legs need more muscular definition' becomes 'My legs are perfectly normal and my new exercise regime helps them become shapely'.
- I have an obvious surgical scar/loss of part of my body becomes 'I wear sexy clothes and/or a prosthesis that minimises this aspect of my body and concentrate on the bits of me that are perfect'.

Now do the same with the negative emotions:

- 'I get bored easily' becomes 'Taking up new hobbies helps me meet new friends and develop new interests in life'.
- 'I feel too tired for exercise' becomes 'My new exercise regime helps me slowly but surely improve my overall level of fitness'.
- 'I keep putting things off' becomes 'I resolve to do things quickly so I'm on top of life rather than life being on top of me'.
- 'I need constant reassurance' becomes 'I am confident in my own abilities and don't need anyone's reassurance but my own. I am good enough'.
- 'I no longer feel sexy' becomes 'I am a sensual and sexual person who deserves a fulfilling sex life'.
- 'Nobody could love me' becomes 'I am easy to love'.

- 'I feel angry at what has happened to me' becomes 'I am leaving my anger behind and moving on – this experience helps me grow as a person and I treat it as a challenge rather than a threat'.
- 'I keep pushing my mate away' becomes 'I accept my partner's love and affection as their support will help me win through this challenging time.'

And so on. The power of positive thought should not be underestimated. If you feel negative about aspects of your appearance or personality, your self-esteem – and relationships – will suffer. Every day, read the lists of good things you wrote down about yourself and say the new positive statements out loud to reinforce your motivation to change. This will change your negative patterns of sub-conscious thought into positive ones that will help you shed your inhibitions and help to revitalise your love life.

There will be some parts of you that can't be changed – such as scars from surgery, or marks left by injuries. These are parts of you and need to be accepted as normal – for you. By learning to love these parts of your body, you can significantly improve your body image and self-esteem.

4 Low Sex Drive

Thanks to the publicity surrounding Viagra, we would all be forgiven for believing that erectile dysfunction (impotence) is the most common sexual problem needing treatment in later life. It is not. Although impotence affects an estimated one in ten adult males, a low sex drive is by far the greater problem and is now the biggest single reason for consulting a sex therapist. In various surveys, loss of libido has been found to affect 30 per cent of middle-aged women, rising to 72 per cent of postmenopausal women. In men, 60 per cent of those feeling stressed will experience a loss of sex drive, while 45 per cent of those with symptoms due to an enlarged prostate gland will also develop a reduced interest in sex.

What is the sex drive?

The human sex drive, or libido, is a powerful force that has a profound effect on our behaviour. Two main types of sex drive exist in all of us: the physical libido, in which there is an aggressive, testosterone-driven need to find a sexual mate, and the psychological libido which is the more receptive, passive, oestrogen-driven willingness to receive the sexual overtures of a potential mate. Although we usually think of males as displaying the more aggressive sex drive, and females the more passive sexual behaviour, this is not always the case. We all have some degree of each sex drive within us and the relative balance between the two can change throughout life.

Traditionally, men are said to reach their peak physical sex drive in their teens, while their psychological sex drive peaks after the age of 50 when testosterone levels fall. Women are said to reach their physical sexual peak in their thirties or forties while their psychological sex drive reaches its maximum in their fifties, at the same time as that of males. This suggests nature has designed things so the relationship between a male and female couple is at its very best during later life when the need to reproduce is less strong.

Variations

Sex drive varies considerably from person to person however, and also from time to time. Some people are driven by a powerful libido that means they seek sexual release at least once a day. For others, sex drive is satisfied by sexual intimacy occurring once a month or less. As long as you and your partner are both happy with the frequency at which you make love, you should consider your sex drive to be normal for you. Too often however, one partner develops a low sex drive, while that of their partner remains unchanged. This frequently causes problems in a relationship, with the partner having a lower libido feeling pressurised, and the other feeling neglected or unloved.

As sex is such a basic survival activity, the pleasurable sensations involved originate in a relatively primitive part of the brain. Unfortunately, this part of the brain is not designed to 'remember' sensations and, as a result, it is difficult to remember feelings of pleasure – just as it is difficult to remember the sensations involved in pain. The memory of sexual pleasure therefore fades quickly, and this can be a major problem when low sex drive sets in. Because you can't remember how wonderful sex feels, there is little reason to want to experience it again. One way round this is to use your sense of smell. Smell is also activated in primitive parts of the brain and has a powerful, evocative effect on memory. Whenever you make love, use a particular, self-chosen blend of aromatherapy oils. When you want to boost your sex drive in the future, smell this particular aromatherapy blend again to help trigger memories of the sensations and feelings involved.

Sex hormones and sex drive

The human sex drive is controlled through complex interactions between sex hormones (eg oestrogen, progesterone, testosterone), certain metabolic hormones (eg prolactin, growth hormone), brain chemicals (eg dopamine) and pheromones – volatile, odourless chemicals secreted in human sweat that have subtle effects on the sexuality of others. Psychological stimuli (sight, imagination), physical factors (taste, smell, touch) and cultural customs or inhibitions also play a role. These interactions are further modified by external factors such as levels of stress, exercise, drug and alcohol intakes, smoking habits, general health, fatigue, diet and even the degree of exposure to sunlight.

The main factors controlling sex drive, however, are undoubtedly the sex hormones, oestrogen, progesterone and testosterone. The level of testosterone is around 20 times lower in women than in men but varies widely. Women who have higher levels of testosterone tend to have a higher sex drive. Testosterone in women is mainly produced by the ovaries so, after the menopause, testosterone levels usually fall although small amounts of testosterone-like hormones (androgens) are also made by the adrenal glands.

Loss of sex drive is the most common sexual problem to affect women, especially after the menopause. Research shows that sexual interest falls off more rapidly in women than men between the ages of 50 to 60 years. By the age of 70, half of all women admit to having little interest in sex, compared with only 10 per cent of men at the same age.

Loss of sex drive is not always due to hormone changes, as it is natural for sexual activity to decline the longer you have been in a relationship. It is important to work out if there are other problems in your relationship, and to ensure you are both still friends. Although it is difficult to talk about an embarrassing problem such as this, it is important to talk about it with your partner. Any frequency of lovemaking is normal so long as both of you are happy about it, and many couples share love, affection and a meaningful emotional relationship without a physically active sex life.

If you still show affection towards each other and you still enjoy a cuddle together, lack of sex drive is unlikely to be due to one or other of you falling out of love, or to problems in your relationship. It may well be linked to your changing hormones, although it can also be linked with tiredness, anxiety, stress or illness.

Drugs and medicines

If you are taking any prescribed medications, it is important to check with your doctor, or a pharmacist, whether these can have an effect on your sex drive. Doctors now accept that at least 150 medicines can affect sexual function in some people. The most common ones are listed below.

Drugs used to treat heart and blood pressure problems

Various types of medication fall into this category, but particular culprits are beta blockers (eg propranolol, atenolol, metoprolol, guanethidine, bethanidine, hydralazine, methyldopa); diuretics (eg bendrofluazide, chlorthalidone, spironolactone) and digoxin.

Tranquillisers

This group includes sleeping tablets and anti-anxiety medications, especially the benzodiazepines (eg diazepam, temazepam, lorazepam).

Antidepressants

Probably the best known group of drugs in this category are the selective serotonin reuptake inhibitors (SSRIs) such as Prozac (fluoxetine) and tricyclic antidepressants (eg amitriptyline). These can significantly reduce sex drive, cause problems with getting and maintaining erections in at least 40 per cent of men, and make orgasm difficult to achieve (and reduce its intensity) in 30 per cent of adults taking them.

Other antidepressants such as trazodone, viloxazine, fluvoxamine, mirtazapine and nefazodone are less likely to affect sex drive.

Other drugs

Some anti-ulcer drugs (especially cimetidine), cholesterol-lowering drugs and corticosteroid drugs (eg prednisolone) can also be implicated in lowering sex drive. So can some antihistamines (eg diphenhydramine, phenylpropanolamine) many of which are also available over-the-counter.

Some of the drugs used to treat prostate problems (eg finasteride, cyproterone) can also cause problems, as can many drugs used to treat cancer.

Opiate pain killers (eg morphine) may also lower sex drive, as may certain antipsychotic drugs such as chlorpromazine or haloperidol.

If you think your low sex drive is linked to a medication you are taking, it is worth asking your doctor if it is possible to switch to another drug or to change the dose you are taking. Do not stop taking your medication except under medical supervision, however.

Other reasons for reduced sex drive

Loss of sex drive can occur in later life for a number of reasons, including:

- familiarity;
- stress;
- anxiety;
- depression;
- lack of sleep;
- pain;
- hysterectomy (see page 105);
- female menopause (see page 61);
- male menopause (see page 52);
- prostate problems (see page 54);

- hypogonadism (see pages 53 and 114);
- prolactinoma;
- lack of sunshine;
- lack of exercise (see pages 4 and 91);
- overweight (see pages 1, 8 and 91);
- low self-esteem and poor body image;
- relationship problems.

Some of these factors, and the way they affect your sex drive, are explored individually below. Information on how alcohol and smoking affects sexuality can be found in Chapter 1.

Familiarity

Once you are happily settled in a loving, long-term relationship, the sensual thrills that accompanied the first flush of love will inevitably reduce, even though your love for each other remains strong. Once the passionate, honeymoon phase is over, lovemaking often becomes less exciting as you become familiar with your lover's body and their tried, tested (and repeated) techniques. If both partners in the relationship are happy with the way things are, there is no problem. If one develops a sex drive that is lower than their partner feels comfortable with, however, this will usually lead to relationship difficulties. Try to keep interest in sex alive by experimenting with different positions and techniques, and varying the time and place of lovemaking so your love life does not become too stale.

Stress

Stress is one of the commonest causes of low sex drive, along with overwork, tiredness and lack of sleep. The adrenal glands usually produce around 5 per cent of circulating sex hormones such as oestrogen and testosterone. When under stress, the adrenal glands produce increased amounts of stress hormones (eg adrenaline, cortisol) instead, so the adrenal boost to sex drive switches off. Stress also causes changes in brain hormones, and in particular increases the output of the hormone prolactin. Prolactin is nature's own contraceptive – it lowers libido and fertility at times when conception is not a good idea.

Unfortunately, stress is common, with many people worried about work, money, health and relationship problems. Reducing stress levels will help to boost sex drive in both men and women whatever their age. Avoid coffee, strong tea, caffeinated drinks, cigarettes and alcohol when you are under stress as these can all make the problem worse. Eat a healthy, wholefood diet and take a good multivitamin and mineral supplement as a nutritional safety net. Relaxation techniques such as meditation, massage, having a warm aromatherapy bath by candlelight and taking time out to rest and relax are essential.

Anxiety

Anxiety affects at least 15 per cent of the population, with 5 per cent regularly suffering from panic attacks linked with over-breathing. Anxiety can lead to physical tiredness, emotional exhaustion and is also linked with loss of sex drive. Breathing exercises, behaviour therapy, counselling and alternative therapies such as homeopathy, hypnotherapy, yoga or meditation will usually help. It is also important to learn to breathe properly.

Signs of a poor breathing habit include:

- rapid, shallow breathing involving the upper part of your chest only;
- shoulders rising significantly towards the ears;
- no visible expansion of the abdomen;
- irregular breathing pattern with lots of deep sighs;
- air gulping which leads to abdominal wind and belching;
- taking deep breaths and holding on to them without breathing out.

These are all signs of hyperventilation and can trigger a panic attack when anxiety is high. To help you recognise what normal, gentle breathing feels like, follow the steps below:

- Lie down and make yourself comfortable and relaxed.
- Rest your hands on the upper part of your chest.
- Feel the way your chest rises and falls as you breathe gently in and out for about one minute.

- Now place your hands on your rib cage so your fingertips almost touch when you breathe out.
- Breathe gently and feel your rib cage moving upwards and outwards for about one minute, concentrating on breathing out rather than breathing in.
- Finally, place your hands on your abdomen with your fingertips just touching.
- Feel your fingers part as your abdomen rises and falls for around one minute.
- Continue breathing gently and hold on to the calm feeling.
- Repeat this breathing exercise daily until you recognise how slow, gentle breathing should feel.

When you are under long-term excess pressure, it is easy for bad breathing habits to build up. By consciously changing the way you breathe, you can help to switch off some of the effects of the stress response and reduce feelings of anxiety.

Quick tips to help stop a panic attack:

- Concentrate on breathing slowly, deeply and quietly to prevent hyperventilation.
- When you feel panic rising say '*stop it*' quietly to yourself:
    - breathe out deeply, then breathe in slowly to fill your lungs;
    - hold this breath for a count of three then breathe out gently, letting your tension go;
    - continue to breathe regularly and gently: imagine a candle in front of your face: as you breathe, the flame should flicker but not go out.
- While continuing to breathe gently, consciously try to relax so that all your tense muscles unwind.
- If panic continues to rise, cup your hands over your nose and mouth so you breathe back some of the excess carbon dioxide gas you have blown off.
- If you are somewhere private, breathe in and out of a paper bag instead.

- Don't escalate the panic by worrying about what is going to happen.
- Try to distract your thoughts by studying your surroundings as you wait for the attack to pass – symptoms usually subside quickly.
- Stay in the situation if practical and you are in no physical danger. If you run away rather than facing your fear, it will be more difficult to cope and to avoid another panic attack when you experience the same situation again.

Depression

Depression affects at least 5 per cent of the population at any one time. It appears to be two to three times more common in women than men, but this may be because men are less likely to admit they have a problem and seek help. The risk increases with age, and women tend to suffer their first depressive symptoms between the ages of 35 and 55 years, 10 years earlier than men.

Loss of sex drive is one of the first symptoms to occur in depressive illness, and one of the last to recover with antidepressant therapy. If you feel your low sex drive is linked with depression, it is important to seek help from your doctor. Other symptoms of depressive illness include sleep disturbance, loss of appetite, low physical and mental energy levels, anxiety, tearfulness and general loss of interest in life around you. If you and your doctor together decide that you need an antidepressant medication, ask whether it is possible to have one that may stimulate your sex drive rather than damping it down further. The antidepressants that are less likely to reduce sex drive (and may even stimulate it) include trazodone, viloxazine, fluvoxamine, mirtazapine and nefazodone.

Lack of sleep

We each spend a third of our life asleep – yet four out of ten people do not get a regular good night's sleep, and 60 per cent of adults experience some degree of insomnia on a regular basis. This can cover a number of different patterns: difficulty falling asleep, waking in the middle of the night and not being able to get back to sleep, sleeping fitfully, or waking up still feeling tired because sleep was not restorative. Lack of sleep can have a serious dampening effect on sex drive, so it is important to try to solve sleep problems when they occur (see page 19).

Pain

Not surprisingly, physical discomfort when making love can lead to lack of interest or even aversion to sex, especially in females. For women, pain when making love may be superficial (eg due to thrush or other genital infections, allergy to spermicides, urethral sensitivity, cystitis or dryness) or deep (eg due to pelvic inflammatory disease, endometriosis, ovarian abnormalities or prolapse of the uterus). Pain during sex is not normal, and medical advice should always be sought without delay. Sometimes using a water-based lubricant such as KY jelly is all that is needed. Soothing washes that help to maintain the acid balance of the female genitals can also help (eg Lactacyd). Avoiding bath products and soaps may also help. If pain during sex is persistent, it is important to seek medical advice.

Pain can also occur during sex due to joint and muscle problems or from other medical conditions that are exacerbated by making love – either through pressure, touch, movement or body position. You can usually obtain useful information and advice on aspects of making love from self help groups, especially on the Internet, so it is worth carrying out a Google search.

It is estimated that as many as three out of four people with long-term pain experience some form of sexual problem as a result. If you have been avoiding sex because of pain, it is important to try to resume a normal sex life as soon as possible – this doesn't have to mean penetrative sex. There are many ways to give and receive pleasure – even a good old-fashioned cuddle and kiss with the person you love can make all the difference to how you and your partner feel inside. You can also use a vibrator or take part in mutual masturbation or oral sex together – as long as you both feel comfortable doing so. If you suffer from long-term pain, you may need to plan ahead so you can enjoy sex at a time when your pain is likely to be at its lowest point. Some people feel better in the morning, for example, while others are less disabled by pain in the afternoon or evening. If there is a time when you know you are likely to feel less stiff, tired or low, then schedule in special time with your partner for then. Remember to plan your sexual activity for a time of day when you generally feel your best. If you are taking medication for pain, try and time your sexual encounter when your medicine is at its optimal peak. Take your pain medication beforehand so you know it will be working at its best during this time. If you find your medication affects your sexuality, then do discuss this with your doctor. It will usually be possible to switch to another form of pain relief which is less likely to cause sexual problems.

Prolactinoma

Raised levels of prolactin occur in 70 per cent of people with a benign tumour (chromophobe adenoma or prolactinoma) of the pituitary gland. The first symptom is often a total loss of sex drive, although unexpected milk production from the breasts (male and female) occasionally occurs as well. It is estimated that between 3 per cent and 8 per cent of men with low sex drive and impotence have raised levels of prolactin. It is therefore important to get your levels checked if low sex drive continues for more than 3 months. If diagnosed, this can be treated with a drug such as bromocriptine which decreases prolactin secretion. Sometimes surgery is required as well.

Lack of sunshine

Many older people have little exposure to natural sunlight. As well as having an adverse effect on the bones by reducing production of vitamin D needed to absorb calcium from the gut, lack of sunshine also lowers mood and reduces sex drive. Sunlight has an effect on the pineal gland in the brain to promote desire and the readiness to mate. This may explain why races with the reputation for greatest passion tend to live in the sunniest climes. Sensible exposure to sunshine (using skin protection creams and covering up with loose, light clothing) may therefore be beneficial for your love life.

Lack of exercise

General unfitness and lack of exercise can lower sex drive through several effects on metabolism and hormone balance. In particular, it can lower levels of the master sex hormone, DHEA (dehydroepiandrosterone) whereas regular, brisk exercise for 30 minutes a day can help to boost DHEA secretion. The level of exercise needs to be sustained for a continuous effect however, and is most marked after exercising for at least a month. Exercise also stimulates release of another substance, phenylethylamine, which helps to intensify orgasm. Increasing your overall fitness level will help to boost your sex drive. Don't over-do exercise however: over-exercising for as little as two weeks can lower testosterone levels by a third. These effects can take three months to return to normal when over-training is stopped.

Overweight

At least one in two Western adults are now overweight (10 per cent above the ideal weight for their height), and a further one in five are obese (20 per cent above ideal weight). Being overweight or obese frequently leads to sluggishness, low energy levels, lack of self-esteem and low sex drive. Excess consumption of carbohydrate causes raised levels of serotonin in the brain which also has a strong, libido-lowering effect. In contrast, losing excess weight can boost your sex drive. Weight loss reduces levels of serotonin in the brain which helps to boost sex drive as body image and self-esteem improve.

Low self-esteem and poor body image

One of the most inhibiting factors when it comes to making love is lack of confidence in your body shape. Women who feel their breasts are the wrong size, their tummy too big, or their thighs or bottom too large have been known to go to extraordinary lengths in order to avoid sex. In one survey, 25 per cent of women were unhappy with the size of their breasts, over 40 per cent were unhappy with their bottoms, thighs or stomachs, and this was felt to have a negative effect on sexuality. Males may also have low self-esteem as ageing changes their body – whether shrinking in some parts or expanding in others. Taking exercise, getting fit and losing excess weight will improve self-esteem, but it is important to learn to accept and even love your body as it is now (see the closing section of Chapter 3).

Relationship problems

Low sex drive can result from relationship problems, where someone has simply fallen out of love with their partner and no longer find them sexually attractive. Hidden anger can also play an important role, especially where the couple find it difficult to communicate. There may also be unresolved issues regarding sexual orientation. Serious relationship difficulties should always be addressed with sexual or relationship therapy such as that offered by Relate (see page 169), if the couple want to stay together. Sometimes splitting up is inevitable, and counselling can help make separation amicable and easier to accept without undue guilt.

5 Female Sexual Problems in Later Life

Many women find that sex feels different in later life from the way it felt when they were younger. This is due to lower levels of the female hormones, oestrogen and progesterone, which can lead to a number of physical and psychological changes that affect your sex life. Not surprisingly, these changes can lead to relationship difficulties as it can be difficult for your sexual partner to understand what you are experiencing. The important thing is to communicate – don't be afraid to let your partner know how you are feeling.

Although sexuality plays such an important role in quality of life, our youth-oriented society often ignores the importance of emotional and physical intimacy in later life – especially for women. Few doctors raise sexual issues during consultations with women who have been through the menopause, yet lack of oestrogen can cause considerable sexual problems and mean that older women are less likely to remain sexually active. One study involving 448 women aged 60 or over found that only 56 per cent of those who were married were still sexually active. There was also a significant decrease in sexual activity with increasing age. Hormone changes occurring as a result of the menopause are frequently to blame. When 39 women were followed from around the time of the menopause until one year after their last menstrual cycle, researchers found that, while all the women were sexually active at the start of the study, only around 50 per cent were still sexually active by the end of the study. A large review of 16 studies of female sexuality after the menopause found that women experience a consistent decrease in sexual interest, frequency of sexual activity, frequency of orgasms and in lubrication after the menopause.

Low sex drive

Loss of desire for sex is the commonest type of female sexual dysfunction and is often the hardest to treat. Low sex drive can be due to a number of factors (see Chapter 4), but in older women it is often linked with falling levels of the hormone testosterone. Even though testosterone is commonly known as the male sex hormone, women produce small amounts in their ovaries and adrenal glands. Women with a higher testosterone level may experience increased desire compared with women with lower testosterone levels. Testosterone levels in women aged 40 years are around half the level found in women 20 years younger. After the menopause, levels of testosterone fall further, along with the hormones oestrogen and progesterone. This may account for low sex drive in some older women, as part of the so-called female androgen deficiency syndrome. Some experts have suggested that low, 'non-masculinising' doses of testosterone might help older women regain their interest in sex, and some doctors are prepared to prescribe testosterone (as implants, patches or in an ointment) to menopausal women along with normal hormone replacement therapy (HRT). This has been shown to increase sex drive, and provide greater satisfaction, pleasure and more intense orgasm. Possible side effects include acne, unwanted hair growth and deepening voice. Excessive doses may also produce flushing, sweating, vaginal itching and clitoral enlargement. The prescribing of testosterone hormone to women remains controversial. Some doctors are against it, while others feel more research is needed to understand the possible beneficial interaction of testosterone and oestrogen after the menopause.

Physical problems

Vaginal dryness

Lack of oestrogen can lead to vaginal dryness which affects every woman to some extent after the menopause. Vaginal dryness usually comes on a year or more after a woman first develops other menopausal symptoms such as hot flushes. Over half of all women develop such a degree of vaginal dryness and lack of lubrication after the menopause that they need treatment for it.

One method of treating vaginal dryness is with the vaginal oestrogen ring (Estring). This is convenient to use, unlike long-term treatment with oestrogen creams and pessaries which many women find messy and unacceptable. Once in place, the vaginal oestrogen ring delivers a small, steady dose of oestrogen exactly where it is needed. There is no vaginal discharge, apart from the natural lubrication encouraged by oestrogen replacement. The ring is left in place for three months, and then replaced – either by a doctor, nurse or by yourself if you are happy to do this. Some women prefer to remove the ring before making love and then re-insert it afterwards themselves, although this is not usually necessary as nine out of ten partners are unable to detect it during sex. If the ring falls out initially because you are too dry, an oestrogen cream can be used for two weeks then Estring can be refitted. This makes insertion and retention much easier. Estring does not dissolve or disappear – it needs to be removed and/or replaced after three months. Lubricants such as KY jelly will also help. Some doctors are now also prepared to prescribe oestrogen replacement tablets or patches to women who have previously had breast cancer – usually where their tumour is known to be oestrogen-receptor negative. Another possibility is to use testosterone to improve libido and sexual response (see page 94).

Lack of lubrication is linked with problems in becoming aroused, as oestrogen is needed to switch on secretion of vaginal lubrication. Sex may also become uncomfortable or painful, and may even result in bleeding from thinning tissues. In most cases, using a special water-based lubricant gel (such as KY jelly or ReplensMD) or pessaries will have an enormous beneficial effect. These are widely available in chemists and supermarkets. In most cases, using a local oestrogen cream/gel will reverse and overcome vaginal dryness – your doctor can advise on whether or not this will suit you. A natural form of vaginal oestrogen replacement, which also supplies useful lubrication, is now also available in the form of an isoflavone gel (called PhytoSoya) which contains plant-based, oestrogen-like hormones.

Painful sex

If you experience discomfort when making love you should always seek medical advice, otherwise it might progress and have a major effect on your sex life. In most cases, discomfort can be solved with proper investigation and treatment, yet as many as one in three women attending sexual health clinics and one in ten attending family planning clinics admit to sexual problems such as pain without seeking help.

There are two sorts of painful sex in women:

- superficial (in which pain is felt near the entrance to the vagina);
- deep in which discomfort is felt deep within the pelvis.

Superficial discomfort in older women can result from infection (eg Candida, thrush), bacterial imbalance (bacterial vaginosis), lack of lubrication and thinning of tissues due to lack of oestrogen. In some women, the hood covering the clitoris becomes pulled back. This exposes sensitive tissues full of nerve endings that may make sexual stimulation intensely unpleasant, especially if there is also a lack of lubrication. If this happens, don't be afraid to confide in your doctor. Oestrogen replacement therapy in the form of vaginal cream, pessaries, ring or vaginal tablets will quickly solve the problem.

Deep pain during sex may be felt during thrusting and is commonly due to the penis hitting an ovary, which is just as sensitive as a male testicle. Experimenting with changes in sexual position (eg woman on top, side by side) may solve the problem. If not, operative tethering of the ovary out of the way (using keyhole surgery) may be required. Other possible causes of deep pain during sex in older women include pelvic inflammatory disease, fibroids and ovarian cysts. Occasionally, painful sex is due to prolapse of the bladder, the rectum or the womb so that they bulge into the vagina. In this case, you may notice a sensation of a lump or 'something coming down'. It can also cause urine to leak from the bladder, especially when you cough. If you suspect you have a prolapse, do consult your doctor. Several treatments are available including pelvic floor exercises, physiotherapy or surgery.

Occasionally, pain when making love is caused by spasm of vaginal muscles due to tension or fear of discomfort – a condition known as vaginissmus. This is not common in older women, yet it is all too easy for doctors to assume female discomfort during sex is psychological. Don't be fobbed off with this diagnosis until all necessary investigations have been carried out.

Treatment depends on the cause. Infections usually need antibiotic or antifungal treatments, lack of lubrication usually responds to a vaginal lubricating gel or local hormone replacement therapy (eg cream, pessaries, ring).

Difficulty reaching orgasm

One in six older women notice it becomes more and more difficult to become aroused and to reach orgasm. This is due to a combination of factors, including lack of lubrication, lowered sensitivity of the clitoris and thinning of tissues which affects the way the vagina lengthens and tightens during arousal. There are also changes in the way the nerves conduct messages which mean that orgasm is more difficult to achieve, and when it does occur, sensation is less intense – this is also linked to weakening of pelvic floor muscles and stress incontinence.

A study in which ultrasound probes recorded what happened during intercourse in women found that when the male penetrated a woman from behind or the side, she achieved a better orgasm than in the missionary position. So it is worth trying different positions until you find one that suits you best at this particular point in your life.

Changes in sensation

Older women often notice changes in skin sensitivity as a result of lower oestrogen levels. In one study, six out of ten postmenopausal women noticed skin numbness so that caresses from their partner were no longer enjoyable. Not surprisingly, nine out of ten of these women found this sensory loss interfered with their enjoyment of sex. Age-related changes in other sensory organs can also affect sexuality. These changes include dryness of the eyes, vagina and mouth, a reduced sense of smell and perhaps a lessening of the ability to detect sex pheromones – the odourless chemicals that play an important role in human interaction and sexual attraction. These changes fade the ability to detect sexual signals and also contribute to loss of libido and the decrease in intensity and importance of sexual function. These changes are often hormone-dependent and may improve if you are able – and willing – to take hormone replacement therapy.

You may find that your skin sensitivity improves if your partner gives you a sensual massage using a blend of sensual aromatherapy oils (eg rose, jasmine, sandalwood, ylang ylang). You may also find it helps to moisturise the skin from the inside by taking evening primrose oil supplements and following a diet rich in plant hormones known as isoflavones (see page 64).

Urinary symptoms after intercourse

There are two main types of urinary problem linked with lovemaking. These are cystitis, and a form of urinary leakage known as stress incontinence. Both can be triggered by sexual intercourse and, not surprisingly, this can put many women off making love.

Cystitis

Cystitis is an inflammation or infection of the bladder which affects as many as one in two women at some time during their life. Cystitis is more common in women than men as the passage leading from the bladder to the outside world (urethra) is much shorter in females (2cm) than in males (20cm) so it is easier for infection to reach the bladder – especially in later life when tissues have thinned due to lack of oestrogen. In most women, the urethra opens above the entrance to the vagina, just beneath the clitoris. In some, however, the urethra naturally opens inside the vagina which makes recurrent cystitis more common.

The symptoms of cystitis depend on the severity of the infection. In mild cases, only one or two symptoms may occur. In severe cases, a sufferer may develop every symptom. These include:

- burning, stinging or discomfort on passing urine;
- a need to rush to the toilet;
- passing frequent, small amounts of urine;
- low abdominal pain or tenderness;
- backache;
- unpleasant smelling urine;
- cloudy urine;
- bloodstained urine.

An untreated bladder infection can spread upwards to infect the kidneys resulting in the more serious condition of pyelonephritis. This usually results in fever and sometimes uncontrollable shaking (rigors).

There are two main causes of cystitis symptoms, infection of the bladder and friction or chemical irritation of the urethra.

Infection is usually due to bacteria from the vagina or bowel. Seventy per cent of cases are due to the bacterium, Escherichia coli, which normally lives in the large intestine.

Sexual intercourse is one of the commonest triggers of cystitis, as it can push bacteria up into the urethra. This is sometimes referred to as honeymoon cystitis. Research suggests that sexual activity increases a woman's risk of a urinary infection as much as fourteen-fold.

Some attacks of cystitis are thought to be caused by wearing tight trousers or nylon tights. This increases warmth and humidity which encourage bacterial growth.

If you suffer from recurrent cystitis, you will need to be investigated for conditions such as diabetes, anaemia and anatomical abnormalities of the urinary system.

Symptoms of cystitis with no evidence of infection is known as urethral syndrome. This is usually due to friction or chemical irritation of the urethral opening which can also cause symptoms of urgency, frequency and dysuria (pain on passing water). Urethral syndrome in later life is often linked to sexual intercourse, too.

Detergents and perfumes can cause a chemical irritation of the urethra or may trigger an allergic reaction. They can also make a bacterial infection more likely by upsetting the normal acidity of the vagina.

Treating cystitis

As soon as symptoms of cystitis start, drink a pint of water. Then drink half a pint every 20 minutes for the next three hours if you can. Fluids help to flush the urinary system through and you will soon start passing water regularly. This may sting at first but will improve as you continue to empty your bladder. It's best to drink water but milk, weak tea, herbal tea or other bland fluids will do. Avoid acidic liquids such as cola, fruit juice or alcohol, which may irritate inflamed tissues.

Unless you suffer from high blood pressure or heart trouble, take a teaspoon of sodium bicarbonate dissolved in water every hour for three hours. This makes the urine less acid, relieves discomfort and helps to stop bacterial growth.

Taking a painkiller such as paracetamol, cuddling a hot water bottle and resting with your feet up will also help. Seek medical advice if:

- symptoms last longer than a day or keep recurring;
- your urine is cloudy or stained with blood;
- you develop a fever or uncontrollable shakes.

Take a sample of urine with you when you visit the doctor – this will be sent off to the hospital to identify the cause of any infection. In the meantime, you will usually be started on a course of antibiotics to which a urinary infection is most likely to respond. By the time the result of your urine test is available, it is likely that your symptoms will have cleared. If they have not, you may need to take another type of antibiotic if your urine contained bacteria that were resistant to the first treatment you were prescribed.

To help prevent recurrent cystitis, wear loose fitting clothes, cotton underpants and stockings instead of tights. Try using panty-liners and changing them frequently

Don't put off answering a call of nature because you are too busy. When sitting on the toilet, try tilting your pelvis up so your back passage is lower than the urethra. After passing water, lean forwards to squeeze out the last few drops of urine. Be sure to wipe your bottom from front to back only. Wash with warm, unperfumed, soapy water after every bowel movement and after making love. If you do not have a bidet, you may find it helpful to pour warm soapy water down between your legs (using a bottle) while you are sitting on the toilet.

Avoid using bubble-bath and other bath additives. Avoid vaginal deodorants, perfumed soap or talcum powder and never douche.

Try to drink at least 2 litres of fluid per day.

Drinking cranberry juice daily can almost halve the risk of developing cystitis. Research involving 153 older women found that drinking 300 ml cranberry juice per day for six months almost halved the chance of developing pus cells in the urine. If pus cells did develop, the chance of them still being present after one month was only 27 per cent of the risk in those not drinking cranberry juice. Further studies suggest cranberries contain substances that prevent bacteria from sticking to the urinary tract wall.

Supplements containing natural extracts of the herbs dandelion, bearberry and peppermint which have an antiseptic and diuretic action are also effective. In one study, 57 women who had suffered at least three episodes of cystitis during the previous year were divided into two groups and given either the herbal extracts or inactive placebo. After 12 months, none of the women taking the herbal extracts had developed cystitis symptoms while almost a quarter of those taking the inactive tablets suffered at least one episode.

Stress incontinence

Urinary leakage due to stress incontinence affects at least six out of 10 post-menopausal women. It is not just a problem of later life, however. One survey found that one in ten women aged between 15 and 64 admitted to wetting themselves at least twice a month. Despite its name, stress incontinence is a physical rather than a psychological problem. It is due to weakness of the pelvic floor muscles, usually as a result of childbirth. It is especially common in women who have had difficult or multiple labours, but is also linked with general unfitness, overweight and the particular anatomy you have inherited. While stress incontinence can cause problems at any stage of adult life, symptoms tend to worsen after the menopause when lack of oestrogen causes female tissues to thin.

Weak pelvic floor muscles mean that the neck of the bladder is no longer supported as well as usual, so it starts to sag. Sometimes, the bladder also bulges into the front of the vagina, causing a pouching known as a cystocoele. This lack of support places strain (ie stress) on the natural valves keeping the bladder closed, so that a sudden increase in intra-abdominal pressure during lifting, coughing, laughing, sneezing or running results in urinary leakage. It also commonly occurs during or after making love. Some cases are mild, with only slight damping but a few women are devastated by a total loss of bladder control which, not surprisingly, puts them off having sex at all. Many women cut down on their fluid intake in an attempt to 'dry' things up. In fact, this usually makes things worse. Urine becomes concentrated, more irritant and is more likely to produce a detectable smell. It is important to maintain an adequate fluid intake of at least 2–3 litres per day.

Treating stress incontinence

Unfortunately, there are no satisfactory drugs available for treating stress incontinence, although drug treatments for overactive bladder (in which symptoms of urinary frequency and urgency occur with or without involuntary incontinence) may help where the bladder is thought to be over-sensitive. If you are able to take hormone replacement therapy (HRT), this will help to return your tissues to their pre-menopausal state and will help to cure mild cases of stress incontinence, as well as increasing the chance of success with exercises or surgery. If HRT tablets or patches aren't suitable for you, you may benefit from the oestrogen vaginal ring or oestrogen vaginal tablets which supply oestrogen locally to vaginal tissues with little being absorbed into the circulation. The older oestrogen creams are also available, but many women find them too messy for regular use.

If you have pure stress incontinence, you will usually be referred to a physiotherapist or incontinence adviser to learn pelvic floor exercises (often known as Kegel exercises after the doctor who first described them in 1948). These exercises are designed to strengthen the pubo-coccygeal muscles supporting the bladder, vagina and rectum. There are two types of muscle fibre involved:

- slow twitch fibres – which need multiple repeated contractions to retrain them;
- fast twitch fibres – which need maximum 'squeeze' effort to retrain them.

For example:

- Pull up the front and back passages tightly as if trying to stop your bowels from opening.
- Hold tight for a count of four and repeat as often as recommended.

Once you have been taught the exercises to do, you will need to practice them several times a day, little and often – some contractions will be quick short ones, while others will last up to 10 seconds. These exercises can be done virtually anywhere and are undetectable. These simple measures can produce a dramatic improvement in 30–70 per cent of women. You should also pull in your pelvic floor muscles before coughing, sneezing or lifting and avoid standing for long periods of time (see also page 42).

It is important to ensure that the right pelvic floor muscles are being exercised. Quality, rather than quantity is the key. It is better to do the exercises well twice a day, than to do them badly ten times a day. Some women find it difficult to identify the muscles involved – in which case you may be shown how to insert one or two fingers into your vagina so that you can practice squeezing these until you can recognise which muscles are involved. Incontinence advisers may suggest a course of biofeedback, in which a probe is gently inserted into the vagina to measure muscle active. This helps to show women when they are contracting the right muscles, and how their strength of contraction can increase.

Sometimes, weighted cones are advised to help boost the effects of pelvic floor exercises. These vary in weight from 5g to 60g and are worn internally for 5–10 minutes a day to tighten and tone vaginal muscles which have to contract to hold the cone in place. They will not suit everyone, however, and are best used under supervision of an incontinence adviser. A more recent innovation is a progressive resistance vaginal trainer device (pelvic toner) which is inserted into the vagina to give the woman something to squeeze against. User trials suggest this can improve symptoms in 42 per cent of women after one week, rising to 79 per cent after one month.

You may also be referred to a physiotherapist who can help strengthen your pelvic floor muscles using a tiny electric current. Two electric pads are placed on the perineum (tissue between the vagina and anus) to stimulate the muscles at regular intervals.

Other treatment options that may be suggested include injecting bulking agents such as collagen around the neck of the bladder (under local anaesthetic) to help support the valve mechanism keeping it closed. Alternatively, you may be offered an operation to help improve support the urinary tube (urethra) or bladder neck. A new technique, known as the *tension-free vaginal tape* operation can now be performed in just 30 minutes as day case surgery, under local anaesthetic or spinal anaesthesia. This allows the surgeon to adjust the tape position to achieve the right level of urinary control for each individual patient. You can usually leave hospital the same day as the level of post-operative pain is low, and follow up studies show that 90 per cent of women are cured or have significantly improved symptoms even five years after surgery.

Most women with stress incontinence can have their condition improved and in many cases solved by one of the measures mentioned above. Unfortunately, half of all sufferers never consult their doctor, either through embarrassment or a mistaken belief that nothing can be done. Do see your doctor. You are not alone. Thousands of women consult their GP about this very problem every month – and wish they had sought help sooner rather than later.

Sex after hysterectomy

As many as 60,000 women have a hysterectomy in the UK every year to treat gynaecological problems such as fibroids, endometriosis, heavy periods, pelvic pain, prolapse or women's cancers.

Many women don't think about how having a hysterectomy may affect their sex life as they are so grateful for treatment to help overcome the problems they are experiencing. But it is worth being aware that the operation might have an effect on your future love life.

Not surprisingly, many women feel depressed or experience feelings of lost femininity and lowered sex drive after hysterectomy. Proper counselling before and after the operation is essential to help avoid this. If you reach your own decision about the necessity for having a hysterectomy, rather than having it forced on you, you are less likely to develop emotional problems. In fact, some woman are so delighted that their pain or bleeding has stopped, the operation literally transforms their life – especially their sex drive.

How long do you need to wait?

Generally, a woman who has had a hysterectomy can resume normal sexual relations as soon as any discharge and tenderness have settled down. Some doctors suggest waiting until after the six week clinic check, although many women wait longer before trying penetrative sex from a desire to allow everything to heal up. The simple rules to follow are:

- take your time;
- use lubricating gels or pessaries to overcome dryness;
- experiment to find which position is most comfortable;
- if anything hurts – stop!

Can the operation affect sexual pleasure?

Many women say their orgasm feels different after hysterectomy. This is because deep muscular contractions occur in the pelvis when you climax. These involve the uterus and some of these sensations will disappear after hysterectomy. Some women find this enhances and intensifies sensations from the clitoris and claim their enjoyment of orgasm is improved – especially if their sex life was virtually non-existent before due to pelvic congestion or constant pelvic pain. For others, however, sensation is decreased. A study in Japan found that 27 per cent of women who had had a hysterectomy noticed the loss of uterine sensations while making love, and that 70 per cent of these had difficulty in reaching orgasm as a result. A similar survey in Finland compared women who had had removal of the whole womb (total abdominal hysterectomy) with those who had just the body of the womb removed, but had the cervix left in place (sub-total hysterectomy). One year later, although researchers found no difference in sexual desire between the two groups, women who had had the sub-total operation experienced significantly more orgasms than women undergoing a total hysterectomy – which may suggest they found sex more pleasurable and therefore indulged more often.

Some researchers dispute these findings, however, and insist that better designed studies have found no difference in sexual function between women who had had hysterectomy compared with those who have undergone other procedures.

Instant menopause

If your ovaries are removed along with the womb during hysterectomy, a sudden fall in oestrogen levels will trigger an instant 'surgical' menopause. Even where your ovaries are left intact:

- one in four women develop menopausal symptoms within two years;
- on average, you will go through the menopause four years earlier (around the age of 47) than a woman who has not had a hysterectomy.

The most likely reason for this is that the operation reduces blood supply to the ovaries.

Sex after the menopause

Many women find sex feels different after the menopause as a result of falling oestrogen levels which have been linked with:

- delayed sexual arousal;
- lack of lubrication;
- painful intercourse;
- delayed orgasm or lack of orgasms;
- painful orgasm;
- urinary problems during or after intercourse;
- reduced sex drive;

- over or under sensitivity of the clitoris;
- generalised changes in skin touch sensations which may make skin contact feel unpleasant.

When 39 women were followed from around the time of the menopause until one year after their last menstrual cycle, researchers found that, while all the women were sexually active at the start of the study, only 50 per cent were still sexually active after one year.

Low oestrogen levels can have both psychological and physical effects on your sex life and can lead to relationship difficulties and low mood. An anonymous survey of female patients registered with four doctors surgeries found 41 per cent admitted to having a current sexual problem. Of these, the most common types were vaginal dryness (28 per cent), difficulty obtaining orgasm (27 per cent), painful intercourse (18 per cent), inhibited enjoyment (18 per cent) and problems with arousal (17 per cent). Overall, almost 1 in 4 women (23 per cent) no longer found sex pleasurable.

In most cases, you will start to feel better as your body gets used to lower levels of the hormone oestrogen.

HRT

Hormone replacement therapy will help to overcome these problems, assuming you are eligible to take it. If you have had a hysterectomy, the doctor will need to know why you needed the operation. He or she will also consider your general health and individual circumstances. After hysterectomy, your surgeon may suggest starting oestrogen HRT either straightaway after the operation, or advise that you wait for six weeks to six months before starting HRT. In some cases, however, HRT will not be advised at all.

Self-help to boost your sex life after the menopause

- Talk to your partner – it can be difficult for them to understand what you are going through. The important thing is to communicate – don't be afraid to let your partner know how you are feeling.

■ Use a lubricant such as KY Jelly or ReplensMD.

■ Check that a low sex drive is not an unwanted side effect of any tablets you are taking – those that can affect your libido include drugs prescribed for high blood pressure, water retention and depression (see page 83).

■ If you smoke, try to stop – research shows that smoking lowers hormone levels enough to bring the menopause on up to two years earlier than normal. It will also affect your sex drive.

■ Avoid excess alcohol. In the long-term, this can lower your sex drive, reduce vaginal secretions, shrink the ovaries and lead to menstrual problems.

■ Avoid excessive stress – take regular time out for rest and relaxation.

■ Take a multivitamin and mineral supplement as a nutritional safety net.

■ Try evening primrose oil for essential fatty acids that help to keep skin soft and supple, as well as providing building blocks for making sex hormones.

■ If you are not taking HRT, herbal remedies that can help overcome menopausal symptoms include isoflavones and black cohosh (see page 63). Seek advice from a medical herbalist.

■ Homeopathic hormones such as testosterone or oestrogen are prescribed by some homeopaths to normalise hormone imbalances associated with loss of libido. Specific remedies such as Phosphoricum acidum or Natrum muriaticum may be more suitable however – seek individual advice from a qualified practitioner.

6 Male Sexual Problems In Later Life

Sexual difficulties are relatively common in older males, but that doesn't mean they are a normal part of ageing, or that you have to put up with them. Medical treatments are now sophisticated and can help overcome sexual problems for most males. If your doctor is unable – or unwilling – to help or answer your questions about sexual difficulties, don't be embarrassed to request a referral to a consultant with a special interest in male sexual health problems.

For a male to enjoy a normal sex life, he must have:

- an active sex drive;
- the ability to achieve and sustain an erection;
- the ability to ejaculate and experience a normal orgasm.

How the penis works

The penis is formed by three cylinders of tissue that run along its length and are responsible for erections. These three cylinders have an internal structure resembling a sponge, and are divided into a series of blood-filled spaces surrounded by small blood vessels, smooth muscle fibres and elastic tissues. The three cylinders are bound together by a tough, outer fibrous sheath known as the tunica albuginea.

When an erection is triggered by physical or emotional stimulation, the smooth muscle fibres in the penis relax so the blood filled spaces become larger and arteries supplying the erectile tissues dilate. As a result, six times more blood starts flowing into the penis and its spongy tissues rapidly expand to press hard against the fibrous tunica albuginea. This squashes the drainage veins running just beneath it so blood cannot escape. Blood therefore remains trapped in the engorged penis which now contains up to eight times more blood than when it was flaccid.

To maintain an erection there needs to be a balance between blood continuing to flow into the organ through the arteries, and blood trickling away through the veins.

Impotence (erectile dysfunction)

The most common sexual problem in older men is impotence – referred to by doctors as erectile dysfunction (ED). ED is the consistent inability to have satisfactory sex due to difficulty in achieving or maintaining an erection. It affects an estimated one in ten men overall, and becomes increasingly common with advancing age, so that 40 per cent of men aged 40 and almost 70 per cent of those aged 70 years are estimated to have some degree of erectile difficulty.

Impotence has a serious effect on a couple's relationship. Over 20 per cent of sufferers blamed erectile dysfunction for the break up of their relationships, yet many men avoid seeking help due to embarrassment or a fear that tests will be invasive or uncomfortable. In most cases, however, only simple questions and a brief physical examination are involved, and often the only investigations needed are measuring blood pressure and simple urinary and blood tests.

The treatment of physical ED has recently been revolutionised with the introduction of new therapies such as locally acting medications and a tablet to take by mouth. As a result, more couples are prepared to seek help and are discovering that increasing age does not have to mean the loss of intimacy in their relationship. The increased awareness about new treatments for sexual difficulties also makes it easier to discuss these problems with your doctor.

What causes ED?

As it is popularly assumed to be a psychological problem, many people are surprised to learn that, in four out of five cases, impotence is due to a physical, medical condition. The most common physical causes include:

- tiredness, overwork and stress;
- diabetes;
- vascular disease (including atherosclerosis and leaky veins in the penis);
- side effects of some prescription medicines;
- fibrosis;
- hormone imbalances;
- nerve damage due to spinal cord injury or the side effects of abdominal or prostate surgery;
- some nervous system diseases such as multiple sclerosis, Parkinsonism, Alzheimer's disease and epilepsy;
- smoking, alcohol and drug abuse;
- psychological problems.

Tiredness, overwork and stress

Tiredness, overwork and stress are the commonest physical cause of impotence and it is normal to perform under par in these circumstances. The adrenal glands usually produce around 5 per cent of circulating sex hormones such as oestrogen and testosterone. When under stress, the adrenal glands produce increased amounts of cortisol and adrenaline instead, and this reduces the boost to testosterone production which the adrenal glands normally provide. It is important to find time for rest and relaxation in this case, and to get enough sleep. Another significant cause of reduced sex drive and impotence in stressed individuals is increased secretion of prolactin hormone which acts as nature's contraceptive and anti-sex hormone. Stress also reduces levels of gonadotrophin-releasing hormone (GnRH). This is the 'master' hormone that kick-starts the ovaries and testicles to produce oestrogen and testosterone, and reduces levels of another important sex hormone, DHEA, in the body.

Diabetes

Diabetes is a major cause of erectile difficulties, with up to 25 per cent of all males with diabetes aged 30–34 affected, and up to 75 per cent of those aged 60–64 years. Diabetes is linked with impotence because persistently raised blood glucose levels that occur when the condition is poorly controlled have adverse effects on both the circulation (hastening hardening and furring up of the arteries) and nervous system (damaging nerves to reduce sensation and affect the nerve signals needed to control the onset of erections). If glucose levels are well controlled in the long-term however, erectile problems may be less likely.

Vascular disease

Both arterial and venous vascular problems can cause erectile dysfunction. Of these, the most common is hardening and furring up of the arteries (atherosclerosis) which can reduce blood flow to the penis from middle age onwards. Studies that outline blood flow into the penis using substances that show up on X-ray or ultrasound can help doctors measure blood flow changes in the penis after injecting a drug to induce erection. This will help to identify whether narrowing of the arteries is the cause of impotence.

Leaking venous valves within the penis can also cause problems by stopping blood from pooling within the spongy tissues of the penis. This typically causes an erection that was initially rigid to slowly sag as blood leaks out of the spongy tissues of the penis. This problem can be identified with special tests using substances that show up on X-ray of the penis (cavernosometry).

Some men suffer from both poor blood supply and venous leakage.

Fibrosis

Fibrosis – a build up of scar tissue – can occur within the penis for unknown reasons to produce Peyronie's disease (see page 128).

Hormonal imbalances

Occasionally, a hormonal imbalance may be the cause of impotence, especially if testosterone levels are too low or prolactin levels too high.

If you suffer from impotence, you will usually have blood tests to identify any underlying hormonal problems.

Underactive testicles – known as male hypogonadism – affects around one in 200 men. The causes are many and include pituitary underactivity, high prolactin levels, abnormal development of the testicles including bilateral undescended testes, chromosome abnormalities, enzyme defects, surgery (eg castration, bilateral hernia repair with reduced blood flow to the testes), testicular disease, chemotherapy, radiotherapy, kidney failure, cirrhosis of the liver, excessive alcohol intake, sickle cell anaemia and androgen receptor deficiency in which body cells cannot recognise the presence of testosterone hormone as well as they should. Male hypogonadism results in low sex drive, fertility problems and erectile dysfunction. It may also produce symptoms of a male menopause. Once diagnosed, treatment (eg with testosterone replacement therapy if indicated) will usually correct these symptoms.

Men whose impotence is associated with low levels of testosterone may benefit from testosterone replacement therapy which is available as tablets, capsules, skin patches (applied every 24 hours), injections (some are given two to three times a week, others are given once every 2–3 weeks), implants (replaced every 6 months) or gel. A sub-lingual preparation that dissolves in the mouth is also under development. Beneficial effects usually occur within two weeks of starting treatment. Clinically confirmed low levels of free (unbound) testosterone affects around 1 in 200 men as a result of underactive testicles (hypogonadism). Some doctors believe that middle-aged and older men may develop low sex drive, and lack of zest for life because although they have normal levels of testosterone hormone, their body cells cannot interact with it as well as in youth. They may therefore be prepared to offer testosterone replacement therapy to treat sexual dysfunction, even where the testicles are not functioning below par. Other doctors disagree however, and place more emphasis on improving general lifestyle factors (stress, smoking, alcohol intake) instead.

Testosterone levels and sex drive have also been increased by prescribing GnRH (gonadotrophin releasing hormone) which is usually secreted by the hypothalamus in the brain, acts on the pituitary gland to release LH (luteinizing hormone) and FSH (follicle stimulating hormone) which in turn stimulates testosterone production in the male testes.

A synthetic androgen, mesterolone, is also available as a tablet for treating testosterone deficiency and male infertility.

It is estimated that between 3 and 8 per cent of men with low sex drive and impotence have raised levels of prolactin hormone, which is produced by the pituitary gland. Raised levels of prolactin may occur due to a benign tumour of the gland known as a prolactinoma. Symptoms can include loss of sex drive, erectile difficulties or unexpected milk production from the breasts (male and female). Prolactin level is usually checked if low sex drive continues for more than three months. If diagnosed, this can be treated with a drug such as bromocriptine which decreases prolactin secretion. Sometimes surgery is required as well, however.

Nerve damage

Diseases or injuries that affect the nervous system can cause impotence. This includes men who suffer from severe multiple sclerosis, or who have sustained a spinal cord injury. Sometimes reflex erections can occur but ejaculation is not normally possible without electrical stimulation. Other neurological conditions such as Alzheimer's disease and epilepsy may also be associated with erectile difficulties. Nerve damage occurring as a result of abdominal or prostate surgery (particularly removal of the prostate gland) can also cause problems.

Side effects of prescription medicines

Prescription drugs are a common and reversible cause of impotence. Over 150 medications can affect sexual function in some people. A detailed list of the most common culprits is given in Chapter 4 on pages 83–84.

If you have erectile difficulties and are taking any prescribed medication, do ask a pharmacist or your doctor if the drugs could be at fault as, in most cases, an alternative treatment that does not have this upsetting side effect can be prescribed instead. However, do not stop taking your medication except under medical supervision.

Cigarette smoking

Cigarette smoking is closely linked with erectile failure. A study of over 300 male smokers measured penile rigidity during nocturnal erections and found a clear, inverse relationship between rigidity and the number of cigarettes smoked each day. The more cigarettes smoked per day, the less rigid the erection. In older males, smoking can hasten impotence by damaging blood vessels and triggering hardening and furring up of the arteries. Impotence has also been linked with smoking in significant numbers of younger males, although the reason is not fully understood it is probably related to the action of nicotine on nerve endings that control blood flow changes within the penis.

Alcohol abuse

Even small amounts of alcohol can reduce testosterone production in males, and hasten its conversion to oestrogen in the liver. The effects of excess alcohol are well recognised in the phrase 'brewer's droop' commonly used to describe impotence linked with drinking. Long-term excessive intakes of alcohol in males can lead to reduced testicular activity (male hypogonadism) resulting in impotence, shrunken testicles, a reduction in penis size and loss of pubic hair. The intakes that can trigger these problems vary from person to person, depending on how your metabolism handles alcohol and how much exercise you take. Sensible drinking levels are no more than three or four units per day for men. Weekly intakes of over 50 units for men are considered dangerous.

Drug abuse

Misuse of drugs – especially alcohol, marijuana, codeine, amphetamines and heroin – can also lead to impotence.

Psychological causes of impotence

Psychological causes of impotence only account for one in five cases, and may be linked with depression, guilt, low levels of dominance and either expressed or suppressed anger. More commonly, psychological problems follow on as a result of the emotional stress of having impotence due to a physical cause.

Treatment for impotence

Fortunately, more than nine out of ten men are able to regain potency with one of the many treatments now available for helping impotence. At present, however, drug treatments for erectile dysfunction are only available at NHS expense under special circumstances. That is to say, they are only available for men with:

- prostate cancer;
- kidney failure;
- spinal cord injury;
- diabetes;
- multiple sclerosis;
- single gene neurological disease;
- spina bifida;
- Parkinson's disease;
- polio;
- severe pelvic injury or radical pelvic surgery including prostatectomy.

However, treatment is also available for:

- men who where already receiving drug treatment for impotence on 14 September 1998 before new restrictions came into place;
- men receiving treatment through specialist services due to severe distress because of impotence.

As these restrictions may change from time to time, do ask your doctor for further information to check whether or not you are eligible for NHS impotence treatment.

Treatments fall into four main groups:

- drug therapy;
- mechanical aids;
- vascular surgery;
- psychosexual counselling.

Drug therapy

A number of drug treatments are able to dilate blood vessels in the penis and encourage erection. These include:

- tablets: sildenafil (Viagra), tadalafil (Cialis), vardenafil (Levitra) and apomorphine (Uprima);
- urethral pellets: alprostadil;
- injections: alprostadil, papaverine, phentolamine.

Sildenafil

Sildenafil (Viagra) was the first oral drug to become available for the treatment of male impotence. It is available in three strengths – 25mg, 50mg and 100mg and is taken around an hour before sexual activity is expected. In some cases, it may start to work within 20 minutes although its effects may be delayed if taken after a heavy meal or after drinking alcohol. Sildenafil cannot be taken by anyone using medicines that contain nitrates (eg for angina).

Sildenafil works by relaxing smooth muscle fibres in the arteries and spongy tissues of the penis. This allows more blood to flow into the penis and more to pool in the spongy tissues inside, resulting in an erection once sexual stimulation starts. It helps three out of four men with erectile difficulties maintain an erection. It is not an aphrodisiac and will only trigger an erection in men who have a healthy sex drive and who are sexually stimulated.

Sildenafil can help men with impotence linked with both physical and psychological causes including diabetes, high blood pressure, depression, spinal cord injury and prostate surgery. In clinical trials, between 70 and 90 per cent of men with erectile difficulties reported an improvement in the quality of their erections, compared with only around a quarter of those taking inactive placebo. This effect was independently confirmed by the men's partners.

Sildenafil is well tolerated although the following side effects have been reported: indigestion, headache, nasal congestion, flushing, visual disturbances (eg mild changes in colour vision and light sensitivity), engorged painful erections (priapism), vomiting and rash. Most reported side effects are mild and do not last long.

Vardenafil

Vardenafil (Levitra) is an oral tablet related to sildenafil and works in a similar way. It is available in three strengths (5mg, 10mg, 20mg) and normally starts working within 25 to 60 minutes. It action is less likely to be affected by eating food or drinking alcohol than sildenafil. It is not an aphrodisiac and does not increase sexual desire – for it to work, sexual stimulation is needed.

Side effects are mild and short lasting. Those most commonly reported include headache and facial flushing.

Like sildenafil, vardenafil cannot be taken by anyone using medicines that contain nitrates (eg for angina).

Tadalafil

Tadalafil (Cialis) is related to sildenafil and vardenafil, and works in the same way. It is available in two strengths (10mg, 20mg) and is longer acting than its two relations. It can be taken with or without food, and preliminary studies suggest it works within 16–30 minutes with the effects lasting at least 24 hours. It can therefore be taken independently of sex, allowing more spontaneity than with other oral therapies currently available. Viagra is usually taken an hour before sex is planned, with effects lasting around four hours, while Uprima (see below) is taken 20 minutes beforehand and generally remains active for up to two hours, so sex requires a certain amount of advance planning.

Some men say their partner prefers not having to see them having to take a tablet in order to have sex – it somehow makes them feel guilty. With tadalafil, the man can take his medication earlier in the day and know it will still work all evening. Many find they can take it one day and still make love next morning, which seems more natural.

Four out of five men taking tadalafil report improved erections, with successful intercourse in three out of four cases – including men with diabetes in whom impotence is sometimes difficult to treat.

Another bonus is that absorption of tadalafil is not affected by food, or alcohol, so a man can enjoy a meal with wine as part of foreplay and still take tadalafil afterwards without worrying that the onset of action may be delayed.

Side effects are mild and short lasting, with headache and indigestion given as the most commonly reported problem. Less common unwanted effects include flushing, stuffy nose, muscle pain, dizziness and backache. Tadalafil is not an aphrodisiac, and does not increase sexual desire – sexual stimulation is needed for it to work.

Who cannot take sildenafil, vardenafil or tadalafil for impotence

Oral treatments for impotence should only be used on medical advice. Your doctor will want to talk to you and assess your medical condition before deciding whether or not a particular treatment is likely to suit you. These drugs cannot be prescribed to men taking other drugs to dilate blood vessels (eg nitrates used to treat angina) as this may lead to a sudden and potentially serious drop in blood pressure. They are also unsuitable for men with conditions in which sex is inadvisable (eg some heart or circulatory problems). Your doctor may advise against them if you have an abnormally formed penis (eg due to Peyronie's disease – see page 128), a disease that might prolong erection (eg leukaemia) or a history of low blood pressure, severe kidney or liver disease.

Apomorphine

Apomorphine (Uprima) is an oral drug for impotence that is taken by placing it under the tongue where it dissolves and is absorbed in about 10 minutes. Drinking a glass of water before using it will help it dissolve. Take care not to swallow it initially or it will not work (though any residual pieces still under the tongue after 20 minutes may be swallowed).

Apomorphine is available in two strengths (2mg, 3mg) and acts in a different way from sildenafil and its relatives. Rather than acting directly on the penis, it acts centrally in the brain to stimulate the nerve signals involved in erectile function. Those taking Uprima are two or three times more likely to achieve an erection than when not taking it, and in those who respond, erections are produced in 10–20 minutes. Its action is unaffected by food.

Uprima should not be used by men with severe unstable angina, recent heart attack, severe heart failure, low blood pressure, and any other condition where sexual activity is inadvisable. Unlike sildenafil, however, it can be used (with caution) in men receiving nitrate therapy. Although Uprima is not classed as an aphrodisiac, some men have found it helps to increase desire.

Side effects are usually mild and short lived. Those most commonly reported adverse reactions include nausea, headache and dizziness.

Urethral pellets: alprostadil

The Medicated Urethral System for Erection (MUSE) is a way of delivering the drug, alprostadil, into the penis without having to inject it. A special delivery device allows a pellet to be inserted painlessly into the opening of the urinary tube (urethra) at the tip of the penis. MUSE is available in four strengths: 125mcg, 250mcg, 500mcg and 1,000mcg. Alprostadil is absorbed from the urethra and works by dilating blood vessels in the penis so more blood flows into the area. Erection usually follows within 5–10 minutes and the correct dose of MUSE produces an erection which lasts from 30–60 minutes. MUSE is effective in almost 70 per cent of those for whom it is prescribed.

The procedure for using MUSE is as follows:

- after urination, the patient lies down, stretches his penis to its full length and slowly inserts the stem of the MUSE delivery system into the end of his penis;
- he then presses the ejector button to release the medication into his penis;
- he slowly and gently rocks the applicator to and fro to make sure the medication separates from the tip of the applicator;
- after withdrawing the applicator, the man – or his partner – then rolls his penis between his hands for 10 seconds to distribute the medication along his urinary tube (urethra).

No more than two doses should be used in any 24-hour period.

Some men experience minor discomfort when inserting the pellet but passing urine beforehand usually overcomes this by moistening the area. In a large trial, 88 per cent of patients rated MUSE as 'very comfortable', 'comfortable' or 'neutral' to use.' Side effects are uncommon but have included light-headedness, dizziness, rapid pulse and swelling of the leg veins. You should not drive for up to an hour after using MUSE. Some men have fainted following the first dose of MUSE, so the first dose is usually given in the doctor's surgery as part of the instructions on use. Because the drug from MUSE enters semen, it should only be used for sexual intercourse with a pregnant woman if a condom is used. Medical advice should be sought before using MUSE with the intention of starting a pregnancy.

Most men for whom oral anti-impotence drugs are unsuitable or ineffective find MUSE preferable to injecting alprostadil directly into the soft tissues of the penis.

Injections: alprostadil, papaverine, phentolamine

Until just a few years ago, the only effective way of giving drugs to treat impotence was through an injection directly into the shaft of the penis. As the drug is given into the cylinders of spongy tissue called the corpora cavernosa, this is known as intracavernosal injection. This method is now less popular with the development of oral treatments and MUSE.

The injection treatment is provided as a sterile powder and liquid (known as the diluent) which must be mixed before use. This is easiest when supplied as double-chamber cartridges.

The drug used, usually alprostadil, relaxes blood vessels and muscles in the spongy tissues so more blood can flow into the penis. An erection will usually occur within 10–25 minutes of giving the injection, and the effects last around 60 minutes.

If too large a dose is given, it is possible to experience a prolonged, painful erection (priapism) so it is important to follow instructions carefully. If this occurs, the usual advice is to exercise vigorously to help the effects of the drug to wear off. If an erection lasts as long as four hours, seek medical advice without delay. If blood remains trapped in the penis for too long it may clot, leading to irreparable damage to blood vessels and permanent impotence.

Some men develop temporary nodules in the penis at the site of injection. These usually disappear but, in a few men, they may become permanent. It may help to vary the injection site slightly.

Although injections are successful in some men, others find the procedure difficult, distasteful and often painful. As a result, around one in three men stop using these injections within six months. Complications can also occur such as bleeding, formation of scar tissue (fibrosis), prolonged erections (priapism) and penile pain.

Mechanical aids

There are two types of mechanical aid that can help impotence:

■ vacuum devices;
■ penile implants.

Vacuum devices

A vacuum device involves placing the lubricated penis in a cylinder and using a pump to create a negative pressure. This allows blood to pool in the penis and, when erection has occurred, the blood is trapped by placing an elastic ring around the base of the penis before removing the vacuum pump. The ring must be removed within 30 minutes. The penis is only rigid beyond the ring, which gives an artificial erection that has been described as cold and lifeless. Some men find the device difficult or uncomfortable to use, and the ring can cause discomfort, especially during ejaculation. Some men have found it impossible to ejaculate with the ring in place.

Penile implants

Penile prostheses are mechanical devices designed for permanent surgical implantation into the penis to produce an artificial erection. Implants are of two main types, semi-rigid rods and inflatable devices.

Semi-rigid rods produce half an erection all the time. They may have an embedded silver wire so they can be bent and 'parked' when not in use, or may have a system of interlocking discs that can be rotated in one direction to lock and become rigid, and rotated the other way to disengage and become flaccid.

Complicated inflatable devices have a small pump that is implanted in the scrotum. A fluid reservoir bag is implanted in the abdomen or pelvis and, on activation, fluid is pumped into the penile segment. Deflation depends on pressing another button so that fluid is pumped in the opposite direction.

Penile implants require open operation but can be very successful. Insertion of an implant takes from 1–3 hours, depending on the type selected. This is performed under a general anaesthetic, or under a local where the body is numbed from the waist downwards (Spinal epidural). It takes around two weeks for the discomfort and swelling of the operation to settle down, especially under the scrotum where the base of the penis is situated. Intercourse can be resumed from 4–6 weeks after the operation, depending on the procedure used. Ejaculation will not necessarily occur.

The main risk with penile implantation is post-operative infection but this seems to be relatively rare. Surveys suggest that 90 per cent of men with an implant are entirely happy with its performance. Most are invisible, although the semi-rigid rods can make the penis stick out a little. This does not look abnormal however. Unfortunately, prostheses have a relatively high failure rate requiring re-operation.

Vascular surgery

Vascular surgery can help to bypass blockages in arterial blood flow to the penis, or correct leaking veins that allow too much blood to drain away from the penis during erection.

If there is a physical blockage to penile blood inflow, it is possible to have an arterial by-pass graft operation in which the blockage is bypassed using a length of vein, or synthetic tubing. In some cases, a single stricture can be dilated with a special balloon inserted into the artery under X-ray control. An alternative approach is to hook up another artery to the penis, which usually delivers blood to the lower abdominal muscles. This is joined to one of the penile arteries using microsurgical techniques and instantly increases the blood flow to the penis. The lower abdominal muscles don't suffer as several other arteries also supply them with blood.

Arterial by-pass surgery involves a fairly large incision extending up the lower abdomen and several days are required in hospital. Some of the penile draining veins are usually tied off at the same time as a bypass operation to increase the effect: this combines better blood flow coming in, with a lesser blood flow draining out. Success rates are as high as 70 per cent. Arterial surgery appears to be less effective in older males – probably because widespread hardening and furring up of the arteries means blood flow into the area is generally reduced. If impotence is solely due to a slow venous leak, this is simply corrected by tying off the major veins draining the penis. This procedure is known as venous ligation, and is successful in 50 per cent of cases. Occasionally, new veins open up after the operation and venous leaking may recur after a few years. Only one in four men undergoing the procedure is able to have normal intercourse more than one year later.

Ginkgo for impotence

Extracts from the ginkgo biloba tree are usually taken to improve memory, but can improve blood flow to the peripheries as well as the brain. The ginkgo biloba, or maidenhair tree, has remained virtually unchanged during the last 200 million years. Its fan-shaped leaves contain a variety of unique substances known as ginkgolides and bilobalides.

Ginkgo extracts relax blood vessels and have a thinning action on blood to improve circulation to the brain, hands, feet and genitals. Ginkgo can improve blood flow to the penis to strengthen and maintain an erection, producing a beneficial effect after 6–8 weeks in men with erectile difficulties. After six months, half of the men taking it had regained full potency.

A study involving 50 males with impotence found that all those who had previously relied on injectable drugs to achieve an erection regained the ability to have spontaneous erections after taking ginkgo for nine months. Of the 30 men who were not helped by medical drugs, 19 regained their erections with ginkgo.

Ginkgo has been shown to strengthen erections in a trial involving 50 males who took ginkgo for nine months.

The standard dose is usually 120mg daily, either as one dose or divided into three. Select extracts are standardised to provide a known amount of ginkgolides (eg at least 24 per cent). Effects may not be noticed until after 10 days of treatment, and it may take up to 12 weeks to have a noticeable beneficial effect.

Seek medical advice before taking ginkgo if you are taking any prescribed medications – especially blood thinning treatment such as warfarin or aspirin. Although at usual therapeutic doses of ginkgo biloba, no effects on blood clotting have been found, research on drug-herb interactions is on-going and some doctors may not recommend combining ginkgo with certain medications.

NB Do not use unprocessed ginkgo leaves from your garden, as these contain powerful chemicals that can cause allergic reactions.

Psychosexual counselling

Psychological or emotional factors are only responsible for one in five cases of impotence. When physical causes have been ruled out, psychotherapy or behavioural therapy can help some men and their partners. It may also help to reduce anxiety and stress in men whose impotence results from another, physical, cause. Your doctor can refer you to a counsellor, or you can contact Relate – the counselling service who offer help to couples experiencing marital and sexual difficulties. In Scotland, this service is provided by Couple Counselling Scotland.

Therapists sometimes advise a form of treatment known as sensate focusing, or pleasuring, to help overcome lack of interest in sex. Information on psychosexual counselling can be found in Chapter 9.

Problems with ejaculation

Premature ejaculation

Premature ejaculation is one of the most common male sexual problems, affecting most men at some time during their life. It is usually defined as ejaculation that occurs before, or within a minute after, penetration. Premature ejaculation is particularly common amongst teenagers and tends to become less of a problem for older males, although it can still occur. It is usually due to anxiety – especially if a new partner is involved. Ways of helping to overcome the problem include:

- masturbating a few hours before starting to make love with your partner;
- wearing a condom to reduce sensations;
- using a local anaesthetic cream to numb the glans penis;
- advising the male to tense his buttocks while thrusting to block nerve signals from the penis;
- thinking of something other than sex to help damp down arousal;

- gently pulling the testicles back down into the scrotum when they rise up to the base of the penis just before ejaculation (but be careful not to twist them);
- using the 'squeeze' technique – in which you squeeze the penis between thumb and two fingers just below the helmet, where the glans joins the shaft (squeeze firmly for five seconds, then wait for a minute before resuming sex – this technique can be repeated as often as you wish);
- after experiencing premature ejaculation, successful intercourse can often occur around an hour later;
- psychosexual counselling.

Retarded ejaculation

Retarded ejaculation is the inability of a man to ejaculate, despite having prolonged intercourse, adequate stimulation, and an intense desire to do so. This is usually associated with tiredness, stress and distraction. In later life, it may also be linked with medical conditions such as diabetes, prostate enlargement, previous prostate surgery and some medications (eg thioridazine, antidepressants, antihypertensives).

Retarded ejaculation may be helped by ensuring surroundings are compatible with unstressful sex – quiet, warm and comfortable with no risk of interruption or being overheard. Avoid overwork, stimulants such as caffeine, smoking cigarettes and drinking alcohol. If problems persist, psychosexual counselling may help to overcome the problem as it is often psychosexual in origin.

Other problems

Peyronie's disease

Peyronie's disease affects up to one in 50 adult males, although many are too embarrassed to seek help. It occurs when some of the spongy, erectile tissues in the penis are replaced with fibrous scar tissue producing a noticeable lump within the shaft of the penis. Why this happens is unknown, but as the fibrous area does not expand during erection, the penis curves – often dramatically – towards the area of rigidity during erection. This gives the erection a distinct banana shape which can be uncomfortable or even painful. Sometimes the bending is so pronounced it makes sex impossible. Although it can happen at any age, Peyronie's disease is most common in men over the age of 50 years.

Some men develop erectile dysfunction as a result of Peyronie's disease – both because of the physical discomfort that erection causes, and because of anxiety about the condition. In around one in ten men with the condition, it will resolve on its own with no treatment. However, if you suspect you may have Peyronie's, it is important to always seek medical advice and have the condition properly diagnosed and treated. As with most conditions, it is easier to treat if picked up early. Having said that, many men with Peyronie's do not need treatment, and will be reviewed regularly by their doctor.

Treatment with vitamin E tablets (at least 200mg daily) is sometimes recommended as vitamin E helps to maintain tissue elasticity. This is controversial however – partly because the condition often improves on its own and it is then difficult to know whether the vitamin E has helped or not.

Some specialists have reported success in reducing pain and lumpiness using the anti-oestrogen drug, tamoxifen. Others have found that injecting a drug called verapamil (usually used to treat high blood pressure) into the thickened area helps to decrease the size of the lump, and reduce discomfort.

Research is also looking at the effects of extracorporeal shock wave therapy (ESWT) to help break up the lump, and initial results look promising.

When intercourse becomes difficult, surgery to elongate the fibrous tissue, or to cut out a wedge from the opposite side of the penis (Nesbit procedure), may be recommended so the erection becomes straight again. The lump is not normally cut out as this can cause future problems with erections. Surgery is only usually considered where the condition has been present for some time and is stable. In advanced cases, implantation of a penile prosthesis may be necessary to maintain erections, however.

Prostate problems

For information on the prostate gland and possible effects on sexual function, see pages 54–58.

Priapism

Priapus was the Greek God of fertility, whose phallus weighed as much as the rest of his body. Priapism describes the onset of a prolonged, painful erection unaccompanied by sexual desire, and which will not deflate. Classically, the shaft of the penis is rigidly erect due to swelling of the corpora cavernosa, while the tip of the penis (glans) and one of the spongy cylinders (corpus spongiosum) remain flaccid. Priapism is painful and may be triggered by certain drugs, injury or any blood disorder (eg leukaemia, sickle cell disease). More often however, it occurs for no apparent reason during sexual activity.

Priapism is a surgical emergency. The penis must be decompressed within four hours, otherwise trapped blood starts to clot and inflammation, scarring and impotence result. Unfortunately, treatment is often delayed as the male is too embarrassed to seek medical help or assumes the erection will go away on its own. Emergency deflation (which should only be performed by a doctor) involves inserting a large needle into the corpora cavernosa and aspirating the thickened, trapped blood which is almost black in colour due to lack of oxygen. Irrigation with saline is then performed and, in stubborn cases, drugs may be injected. If all else fails, the erection is coaxed away by opening the corpora cavernosa and joining them to the corpus spongiosum. This allows drainage, but will prevent any erectile activity in the future without the use of an implanted penile prosthesis.

Male painful sex

There are two sorts of painful sex in men – superficial pain involving the penis and a deeper discomfort often felt in the testicles.

In men who have not been circumcised, pain in the penis that only occurs during sex or masturbation may be due to an over-tight foreskin. This can come on in later life due to thickening or tightening of the foreskin. In severe cases, splitting even occurs. This can often be improved by using a cream containing an antifungal agent plus a weak corticosteroid cream available on prescription from your doctor. If this does not help, you may need to resort to circumcision, though personal lubricants may help.

Soreness of the tip of the penis is often caused by thrush. It can also be due to sexually transmissible infections such as herpes, gonorrhoea or chlamydia which can inflame the urethra (tube leading from the bladder to the outside).

Any soreness of the penis – especially if accompanied by a discharge – should be investigated at a genito-urinary clinic. Don't be embarrassed about going. Your problem will be instantly diagnosed by examining discharge under the microscope. Treatment can then start without delay.

If you experience pain in the testicles during love-making – or at any other time – it is important to get checked out. You might have inflammation of the testicle, it may be twisting on itself or you may have a cyst, lump or hernia. All need medical assessment and diagnosis.

Hernia

Some older males find their sex life is affected because they have developed a hernia. Hernias are common and nothing to be embarrassed about. A hernia occurs when an internal part of the body pushes through a weakness in the muscle or tissues that normally contains it. The most common types of hernia form when part of the intestines pushes through the muscular wall of the abdomen. This forms an external bulge or lump which is sometimes referred to as a rupture. The bulge of an external hernia normally contains a sac made of the membrane lining the abdominal cavity (peritoneum). The sac contains either a loop of small intestine, or a piece of the fatty membrane (omentum) that is attached to the outside of the small intestines. A hernia filled with omentum is less likely to cause complications than a hernia containing a loop of bowel.

A hernia develops at an area of weakness, such as where:

- a structure such as a major blood vessel enters or leaves the abdomen;
- muscles fail to overlap properly;
- there is only scar tissue rather than muscle (eg belly button area);
- a surgical scar or accidental wound has previously cut through the abdominal wall.

A hernia is often triggered when an increase in pressure causes the weakness to give way. This may be due to persistent coughing, lifting heavy objects, or straining with constipation. Being overweight also increases the risk of a hernia as it places greater strain on an area of potential weakness and may also cause it to distend.

The most common hernia to occur in males is an inguinal hernia. The inguinal canal is a natural weakness in the groin, where the abdomen is connected to the top of the leg. This area is weaker in men than in women as it is the passage through which the testicles and their blood supply pass from the abdomen to reach the scrotum. Inguinal hernias, in which intestinal contents bulge into the inguinal canal, are therefore more common in men than in women. As they become larger, they track down towards the scrotum in men, where they can produce a large bulge.

If an external hernia develops suddenly, you may notice a sensation of something giving way, plus some discomfort or pain that usually improves. Otherwise, you may just notice the appearance of an unusu-al bulge or lump appearing in the groin or in the scrotum. The lump will feel soft and usually bulges when you cough. In a reducible hernia, the bulge can be gently pushed back into place and will disappear when you lie down.

If a hernia cannot be reduced – either because it is too large, or because the hole through which it has passed is too narrow – it may become trapped and painful. If the blood supply to the trapped intestine becomes cut off – a condition known as a strangulated hernia – severe pain occurs and you may also develop sign of intestinal obstruction such as vomiting, abdominal pain, distension or constipation. This is a surgical emergency that needs urgent treatment to free the trapped bowel.

If you notice an unusual bulge or lump in any part of your body, it is important to see your doctor for a proper assessment and diagnosis. If the lump is very painful, contact your doctor straight away.

Treatment

An external hernia in an adult will not heal by itself and, if left untreated, may gradually become larger to cause discomfort and dragging sensations. It can also interfere with your love life. Some hernias are also at risk of becoming trapped and strangulating.

The traditional treatment for an external hernia involved wearing a supportive truss, but this does not solve the problem. All it does is provide support over the area of weakness, so the hernia does not come down while the truss is worn. Most men would prefer to have the hernia permanently repaired.

The original surgical repair of a hernia involved pushing the intestines back into place, then strengthening the weakness by stitching the two sides together. These stitches were placed under tension to hold the wound together, which could cause discomfort at first. Up to 20 per cent of these tension hernia repairs will recur in the future.

An American technique is now available in the UK to repair external hernias using an open, tension-free reinforcement. A small incision is made over the hernia and the bulge put back where it belongs. A special, sterile piece of mesh is then placed at the hernial opening and firmly held in place while the wound is closed. There is no stitching directly into the muscle and, because there is no tension, much less post-operative discomfort. The special mesh encourages the growth of strong, fibrous tissue which grows around and through the mesh to strengthen the wound. This quickly develops into a tension-free reinforcement which, because it is inside the abdominal wall, means the hernia is less likely to recur.

The operation is usually performed under local anaesthetic, takes around 20 minutes, and the person can walk away afterwards without needing to rest in bed.

Research suggests that one in five people undergoing this newer procedure did not need pain-killers after the operation, and the average time taken to return to work was nine days for manual workers, and less for those with desk jobs. Only eight recurrences occurred within an 18 month to 5-year follow up. This is 20 times less than with the traditional technique in which nylon thread is used to darn the area of weakness.

If you have a hernia, check which procedures are available in your area to repair it.

7 Loving Relationships in Later Life

A loving relationship is an equal one in which both partners have mutual respect for each other and feel able to talk openly to each other about problems. Good communication, especially when discussing a sexual or relationship problem, means:

■ expressing yourself clearly;
■ being pleasantly assertive to protect your rights without infringing those of others;
■ listening carefully to others: both to hear what they are saying, and to check how well they have understood you;
■ reaching an agreed endpoint where you both know what is happening and how things will progress, if necessary;
■ becoming more aware of other people's needs.

Communication

Expressing yourself

Expressing yourself clearly means saying what you mean, and meaning what you say without using veiled hints and comments. Before you can express yourself clearly, you need to explore your own emotions to understand exactly how you feel about a particular situation. This helps you recognise when an issue needs to be dealt with assertively rather than passively endured.

To express yourself well, you need to choose the right time and place for dealing with problems. Some issues need to be dealt with immediately, as soon as the situation has arisen. Other more long-term problems in your relationship can be addressed after you have had time to understand your feelings about the situation more fully.

Choose a phrase that succinctly sums up what you want to say. Use 'I' language: I feel … I would prefer … I would like … Rather than 'You' language: You must … You should … etc. 'I' language is assertive, while 'you' language comes across more aggressively.

Try to stick to the point, without nagging or getting side tracked. If you are dealing with a problem that annoys or upsets you, then use a formula that states what the problem is (eg You were late home again this evening); How this affects you (eg I was left waiting and dinner is over-cooked); How this makes you feel (eg I felt annoyed and upset); how you would like the issue resolved (eg Please make sure you are home on time in future). This is the desirable endpoint that you are requesting.

Listen to your partner's response to ensure they have understood what you have said, have taken it on board, and agree. If they do not agree, then you may have to agree to differ.

Assertiveness

Both partners in a relationship are equal and have the same basic rights. If you disagree with your partner, you need to say so in a calm, responsible manner. Being assertive is the desirable mid-path between being passive and being aggressive. It allows you to express your thoughts, feelings and needs clearly and openly while recognising those of others, and taking steps to identify and solve potential conflicts within your relationships with others. Everyone has the right to:

- be themselves;
- express their own opinions and beliefs;
- be listened to and respected;
- consider their own needs;
- set their own priorities;
- take responsibility for their own actions;

136

- get things wrong;
- not understand;
- say yes;
- say no;
- disagree;
- be assertive without feeling guilty;
- not be assertive when they choose.

People who are assertive rather than aggressive choose phrases such as:

- I think …
- I would like …
- I would prefer …
- We could …
- Why don't we …
- Let's …
- What do you think?
- Is that OK?
- How do you feel about that?

Assertiveness skills are based on a few tried and tested techniques that give you the verbal tools to say 'no' politely and firmly. This helps you express your rights and can deal with many of the sources of stress in your life.

You may find it surprising how often you have agreed to do something you would really rather not do simply because you did not know how to say 'no'. Even more annoying is when you say 'no' but are then, somehow, persuaded to change your mind and say 'yes' instead. Being assertive means knowing how to say 'no' and mean it. There are some secrets to saying 'no' successfully:

- Avoid using the word 'no' or the phrase 'I can't'. Instead, say 'I am unable to …' or 'I am unwilling to …'
- Remember that by declining, you are rejecting the request, not the person.
- Accept that sometimes you may have to upset someone if you cannot comply with their request – their upset is their problem however.

Don't make it yours by giving in and saying 'yes' when you really are unable to do something.

- Pause before answering a request if you are not sure about it – it is permissible to say 'Can I get back to you on this?' or 'Can I let you know later?'

- Practice saying 'I am unable to …' out loud in private, using a variety of phrases until you find one or two you are comfortable with.

- Acknowledge the other person's need without giving in: 'I understand you need someone to help, but I am unable to do that right now'.

- Be brief. Don't give a long speech about why you have to say no. A non-committal phrase such as '… other priorities I have to attend to …' is more than enough explanation. If you are interrogated about why you cannot do something, you can always reply 'I prefer not to say'. Keep repeating your statements like a broken record if necessary to deflect the other person's insistence.

- Be calm and pleasant. Don't snap. If necessary, thank the person for asking you but still say no. 'No, I'm afraid I'm unable to make that, but thank you for asking me.' 'I understand the importance of what you are asking me to do, but I am unable to do it right now'.

- If they persist and you are finding it difficult to resist, then say so. 'I'm afraid I am unable to do that, and you are making it difficult for me by trying to insist. Please don't.'

- It usually helps to end the conversation quickly. 'I'm afraid I am unable to do that, but thank you for asking me. I don't want to sound abrupt, but I really do have to go now.' This reduces further opportunities to change your mind.

There are several techniques that help you remain assertive yet pleasant.

1 Basic assertion

This involves making a straightforward statement in which you calmly insist on your rights. Use a short statement that clearly sums up your needs, feelings or opinions. If, for example, someone becomes unpleasant because they want you to go on a trip with them on a day when you have made other plans, just say: 'We are unable to go with you next Sunday'. When the person reinforces their argument, you do the same. 'We're still unable to go with you next Sunday.' Never feel you have to explain – don't for example, start telling them exactly what plans you and your partner have arranged for that weekend.

2 The cracked record

This is a simple skill which is sometimes necessary when you need to be persistent to resist someone who is very persuasive. It merely depends on selecting a phrase and repeating it as often as necessary until the other person gives up trying to manipulate you. For example, just keep saying calmly 'We are unable to go with you next Sunday'. Keep repeating your statement each time the other person comes back with another demand or suggestion. If they don't respond after you have repeated your point, stay quiet – being comfortable with maintaining silence is vital as you need to state your case one more time than the other person makes their point.

3 Negotiation

It will usually help to reduce the tension if you can offer an acceptable compromise. 'No, we are unable to go with you next Sunday. However, we could go with you the following Sunday instead. Is that helpful?' Keep calm and breathe slowly, remaining in control. Compromise makes everyone feel better as no one really loses. You have asserted your right not to change your plans at short notice, and have also offered a possible solution to the dilemma.

4 Dealing with recurrent irritations

If your partner repeatedly does something that upsets you, you need to deal with it calmly without causing resentment. It helps to work out a statement in advance that simply describes:

■ the nature of the problem;
■ how it affects you;
■ how it makes you feel;
■ how you would like it resolved.

If, for example, your partner keeps walking into the house with dirty shoes, you could deal with it by saying: 'You keep walking into the house with dirty shoes. This means I have to clean the floor again, which upsets me. I don't mind doing it occasionally, but I feel it is unreasonable for you to keep treading mud through the house. Please wipe your feet on the doormat, or take off your shoes and try to be more thoughtful in future'.

5 Owning up

Asserting your rights also means taking responsibility for your own actions. If you make a mistake, it is important to acknowledge the fact. Say sorry, give your personal commitment that it will not happen again, and learn from the experience. This allows you to retain your self-respect and shows that you have sufficient confidence and maturity to take full responsibility for your behaviour. For example, if you forgot to take an important letter to the post office, say something like: 'I'm sorry. I fully intended to take the letter but I forgot. It's my fault and I will send it by special delivery tomorrow to help make up for it. Do you want me to phone the bank to say why the letter is delayed?'

6 Accepting criticism

Being assertive means being able to accept constructive criticism but defending yourself against unfair criticism. Constructive criticism can be useful, but destructive criticism is something you want to rise above and forget about. It is not always easy to work out which type of criticism it is at the time it is made, however. You may need to go away and analyse what was said, whether or not the person was in a good mood or feeling vindictive, and whether or not they had your best interests at heart. In the meantime, you need to know how to accept criticism so it either helps to clarify whether the criticism is constructive or destructive, or helps you disarm the critic. It is important to stay relaxed, and to breathe slowly, deeply and calmly. Smile, lean slightly towards the person rather than drawing back and don't respond until you've had time to think about what you want to say. The following techniques can help:

- Pause: is the criticism valid: Yes? No? Maybe?
- If the criticism is valid:
  - Agree: 'You're right, I can be untidy, but I'm working on it'.
  - Express thanks: 'Thank you for letting me know', 'That's a useful comment, I'll think about it' or 'I'm glad you told me'.
  - If necessary, apologise: 'I'm sorry. I'll take steps to put that right'.
  - Learn from the criticism.
- If the criticism is invalid:
  - Challenge: 'Why are you saying that?' 'Why do you feel the need to say that'?
  - Ask for specifics: 'Would you mind explaining exactly what I did to make you say that?'
  - Say you disagree with their assessment: 'I'm always willing to hear what you have to say. However, on this occasion I disagree for the following reasons ...' If the criticism is repeated, say something like: 'Clearly we disagree. I still don't feel your criticism is valid.'
- If you are not sure whether or not the criticism is valid:
  - Challenge: 'Why are you saying that?' 'Why do you feel the need to say that?'
  - Ask for clarification: 'Could you be more specific?' or 'What exactly do you mean?'
  - Ask their advice. 'How would you have done things differently?'
- If someone was unkind enough to make the criticism in front of someone else, you could appeal to that person if you feel the criticism is unfair:
  - 'Jane, what do you think? Do you agree?' Or 'Do you believe that's the case?'

Try not to feel hurt. Put downs should only hurt if you believe there is truth in what is being said. If, for example, someone criticised you by falsely saying 'You have purple hair,' this would not hurt at all and you would easily laugh it off. Similarly, if someone says 'You're lazy' this should not hurt if you know it is not true. If it is true, say 'thank you for letting me know' and try to do better.

Remember:

- No-one can make you feel inferior without your permission – they can only invite you to. How you respond is up to you. Believe in yourself.
- Everyone has a right to be wrong sometimes, including you.

Enhancing your relationship

Learning to listen

There are times in a relationship when you need to be a good listener. Being a good listener involves:

- Facing the person who is speaking to you, giving them your full attention and maintaining good eye contact without staring.
- Giving verbal encouragement: use words or sounds such as 'Uh-huh?', 'Really?' 'Yes?'
- Giving non-verbal encouragement: nod your head, animate your face to reflect what you are hearing, eg look sad, happy, interested, amused or frown as appropriate.
- Avoiding interruptions until the person has had their say. Don't be tempted to finish their sentence for them. Be patient and give them all the time they need to express themselves fully.
- Reply appropriately with a phrase that sums up what you have just heard: eg 'That was quite an experience and you obviously feel upset.' Or 'So you're saying you are upset with me because I was late …'
- Make a suitable closing statement: 'Let's go and have a cup of tea while you calm down.' Or 'I'm sorry I've upset you. I'll do my best to ensure it doesn't happen again.'

Coping with sex problems

A discussion aimed at addressing sex problems needs to be frank and open, not hidden behind gestures, inferences, veiled comments, jokes or put-downs. Set aside a time when neither of you are under pressure to do something else, and choose a neutral setting such as the lounge. Don't attempt this after you have just tried to make love or when either partner is feeling rejected, hurt or angry, or it may degenerate into a shouting match.

It is important to be clear in what you are saying, so think about what you want to say beforehand and how you are going to say it. Deal with the most important issue first, and be careful and sensitive in what you say. Try not to express your feelings as a criticism or blame; use 'I' language. For example, rather than saying 'You …' say 'I would prefer it if we …' It is also a good idea to avoid generalisations such as 'You never …' or 'You always …' Aim to be positive – start off with a good point about the topic under discussion rather than going straight in with what is wrong. Try not to criticise each other, or to bring up old grievances that are not relevant to the point under discussion, as it is then easier to work together to find a way round the problem without feeling defensive or aggressive. Similarly, it is important not to talk at your partner, but to give them chance to respond. Take it in turns to make a point and don't move on to the next issue or get side-tracked until the first issue has been resolved. If you cannot agree on ways to approach a particular problem, however, you can mutually agree to put it to one side and come back to it later. If you are feeling hot under the collar, use a pre-arranged signal to take a break and cool off. And if the discussion fails, try writing down your feelings to each other in a letter instead.

Thinking more rationally

Psychologists have identified a number of common errors in the way people think when coping with difficult situations such as relationship problems. Try to avoid:

- Fixing labels: eg 'I'm stupid', 'You're a loser', 'She's an idiot', 'I'm not good enough'.
- Jumping to conclusions: eg 'He must think I'm useless', 'They must think me stupid', 'He must be fed up with me by now', 'I'm

going to fail', 'This won't work', 'There's no point asking, they're bound to say No'.

■ Concentrating on negatives: eg 'Everyone pities me', 'I always mess up'.

■ Downplaying positives: eg 'I was only invited to make up the numbers'; 'I only did that through sheer luck'; 'He only said that to keep on my good side'.

■ Generalising: eg 'Nothing ever goes right', 'That will never work'; 'I always get it wrong'; 'Everyone's against me'.

■ Upping the ante: eg 'This is the worst day of my life'; 'We're on the edge of the abyss'; 'It's killing me'; 'I can't stand it any more'.

■ Accepting inappropriate blame: eg 'Whatever goes wrong is always my fault'.

■ Blaming others: such as 'It's all his fault – he should have warned me'.

■ Minimising events: eg 'I was successful, but I could have done better'.

■ Letting your emotions rule: eg 'I feel stupid, so I must be', 'He made me feel upset, so he must be really horrible'.

■ Making mountains out of molehills: it is common to use words that greatly exaggerate events. Look at the following list of words and try substituting those in the second column for words you commonly use from the column before.

Instead of:	Try using:
Terrible	Inconvenient
Dreadful	Annoying
Catastrophe	Nuisance
Awful	Unfortunate
I ought to	I would prefer to
I have to	I would like to
I must	I intend to

It can help to write down your thoughts and analyse them to see what thinking errors you are making. If you can eliminate these irrational thoughts, you will be able to deal with relationship problems more easily.

- If, for example, you are looking at a situation in black-and-white terms, or are exaggerating things, try to find some middle ground that helps you keep things in better perspective.
- If you find you are putting a label on someone as a result of their actions, is that label really justified?
- If you believe your own performance is poor, are you being too harsh on yourself? Try asking other people for their opinion and use their feedback in a positive, constructive manner, and accept you have done well when you have.

Being aware of the needs of others

It is important to be aware of your partner's needs. It is easy for couples to start taking each other for granted or at least to appear as if they are. Try to:

- Make more time to do things together.
- Find time for fun.
- Look at each other when speaking: put the newspaper or magazine down; switch off the TV.
- Tell your partner you love them regularly.
- Give shows of affection in private – a hug, peck on the cheek, card or small present goes a long way.
- Give shows of affection in public – an arm round the shoulder or holding hands means a lot.
- Share household chores.
- Inquire after each other's day.
- Share successes with your partner.
- Discuss worries with them too.
- Ask their opinion on things that matter to you.
- Avoid criticising them in public.
- Be faithful.
- Respect each other's independence.
- Respect each other's privacy.
- Provide unflagging loyalty and support.

8 Being Alone

Many older people will no longer be in an intimate relationship, due to bereavement or separation from their partner. Some may never have had a long-term relationship and may be used to living a single life.

If your relationship has recently broken up, remember that time is your best friend. In two or three months time you will start to come to terms with the changes in your life, and within 6 months to a year you will feel very different from when the relationship first ended. Don't bottle up your emotions – express your feelings and don't be afraid to cry. Crying is a great way to let out your pent-up emotions and you will usually feel much better as a result. It is important to have someone close you can talk to or confide in – but it must be someone you trust like a close family member or an old friend. If you lack this sort of support system and you desperately need to talk to someone, remember that the Samaritans are always on the end of the phone to listen.

Everyone needs to be loved and wanted, and these needs do not change just because you are getting older. You may find you are seeking other forms of attachment than when you were younger, however. You may prefer to enjoy simple companionship and someone to share your favourite activities rather than a bed partner or someone who lives in the same home as you.

If you miss physical intimacy, however, and wish to find another person with whom to enjoy a sexual relationship, you may feel awkward and embarrassed, not knowing where or how to start. These are perfectly normal feelings, especially if you have been bereaved.

Bereavement

Sooner or later everyone has to cope with bereavement. Whether it is the death of a parent, partner, child, family pet or close friend, the loss of a loved one is a devastating experience that affects your whole life and causes an enormous amount of stress. Everyone will react differently and every situation is different, but grief is a painful and isolating experience. Try not to be alone however – even if you feel you want to shut yourself off from the outside world. Company is important at this difficult time. The support of family and friends is vital. You need to be able to talk about your feelings openly, without holding back. If someone asks how you feel, it is no use saying 'All right' if you feel absolutely awful. Take the opportunity to be honest about your feelings.

Emotional feelings

As well as physical symptoms, anyone faced with death will feel unpleasant emotional symptoms such as shock, panic and helplessness at first. The facts take time to sink in, and feelings of unreality, such as 'It can't be happening to me' or 'This isn't real' are common. You may feel numb, and find it difficult to cry – but it will help to let your emotions out and shed a few tears or even scream and shout. Time is your best friend, as the weeks and months pass, it gets easier to accept what has happened. You may feel guilty, that in some way you are to blame for what happened – again, this is a normal part of the grieving process. Later, you may feel angry at your loss, or jealous of others who have not had to go through what you have had to face. With time, you will start to accept what has happened and look to the future.

A number of emotions are commonly felt after bereavement. These can include:

- numbness and feelings of unreality;
- sadness and longing;
- helplessness;
- fear for the future;

- anger and resentment;
- loneliness;
- disappointment and despair;
- guilt or shame.

These are all a normal part of the grieving process and if you are experiencing them, don't worry unduly. These will soon mature into feelings of resignation, acceptance and hope for the future.

Sharing your feelings

When you are coping with the stress of bereavement, it is important to voice your feelings, and share them with others as this is a powerful part of the healing process.

Thinking and talking about the person who has died will help keep their memory alive for you. To begin with, this can be painful as it will bring raw emotions to the surface, but sharing your feelings is healthier than bottling them up.

Try talking with a close friend or relative – someone who also knew the person who has died – as this will help you both. Some people find it easier to talk to someone removed from the situation, however, such as an uninvolved friend, doctor or a priest. You may even feel that professional bereavement counselling is what you need, either as well as or instead of talking informally. Do whatever you feel most comfortable with.

With time, you will be able to talk about the person with pleasure, remembering all the good times you shared. This is not 'dwelling in the past' or 'failing to get over it'. It is a healthy way of coping with your loss. When you can smile again, you will know you are well on the way to recovery.

Everyone will eventually recover from the raw emotions, stresses and changes that result from a bereavement, but you will need to recover at your own pace and in your own time. Don't rush it as it is important to let the process run its natural course for you. There are no right or wrong ways to grieve, and everyone copes differently. Sometimes, people who have suffered a bereavement slowly sink into depression. Depression can creep up on you, until you are overwhelmed with feelings of sadness, loneliness and despair. If you start feeling that things are getting on top of you, that you can no longer cope, or that life is no longer worth living, it is important to seek help from your doctor. Depression is an important warning sign that the stress resulting from your bereavement is overwhelming and that you need professional help to come to terms with your loss.

The nature of grief

Grief is an intense stress reaction in which you are likely to experience a number of stress-related emotional and physical symptoms. These are all part of the normal grieving process, too, along with feelings of guilt, anger, depression, loneliness and – eventually – hope.

When a loved one dies, it is also common to develop sleep problems. It can be difficult to get off to sleep, and when you do manage to nod off, you may find that your rest is disturbed by unusual dreams or that you wake earlier than normal.

Sleep is one of nature's healers, so it is important to get a good night's rest. If it is your partner who has died, the bedroom will be associated with memories and it often helps to move into the spare room for a while, or – even better – to stay with relatives or close friends. It can even help to phone someone and have a short conversation with a friend or relative before going to bed so you can voice any worries or thoughts that might otherwise stop you sleeping. For hints on how to get a better night's sleep, see page 21.

Starting a new relationship

After a partner has died, there may eventually come a time when you wish to start a new relationship with someone else. When this happens, it is natural to feel guilty as if you are somehow betraying your late partner. You are not. Your life must go on, and you can cherish and enjoy the memory of what you had with your previous partner while still getting to know someone else – once you feel ready. It is a matter of learning to adapt and adjust. You do not have to accept that the end of your previous relationship means an end to all forms of sexual expression unless that is what you actually want.

When you are single, going out on a date can be just as daunting in later life as it was in your teens. You may feel rusty when it comes to small talk and social chit-chat with someone you find attractive, but take things slowly and try to just be yourself. A first date should be a fun time in which both of you size each other up to see if you might want to see each other again and take the friendship a bit further.

If you have a medical condition that affects your sexuality, your ability to have sex, or which has left a visible scar on your body, you will understandably feel self-conscious about this. If the relationship develops to the point of intimacy, it is probably best to discuss any medical conditions you have beforehand if they are likely to become apparent when making love. People with a particular medical or surgical problem often find it difficult to interpret what is said when discussing a topic that makes them anxious, as you may have already formed conclusions about how your partner is likely to respond. This is a defensive position that can get in the way of hearing what is really being said. Any medical condition you have is simply an illness that you have. That is all. It does not define who or what you are. Any new partner worth getting to know better will understand that.

Just like in your teens, not all dates will work out or lead on to further meetings or intimacy. No-one finds it easy to deal with rejection, but in the dating game there are usually more rejections than acceptances, so try not to take them personally. There will be plenty of others – lots of people out there would enjoy your company, it is just a question of being patient and remaining open to new possibilities, until you find the right person. Sometimes it is also a question of waiting for the right time – for you and the other person, too.

Falling in love again

Many single, older people fall in love and enjoy the new emotions that love and intimacy can bring in later life. Your family may seem unsupportive or even shocked, but try not to let them put you off progressing a new relationship. Few people are entirely comfortable with change and the thought of their older relative embarking on a new relationship – particularly one that may have a physical side – can seem challenging to them. They may be unsure of their role in your life, and may even feel sidelined. Their reaction is more to do with them and their attitude than it is to do with you. You must do what you feel is right, in your heart. It is your life and future. Enjoy!

In a long-term relationship, the depth and richness of lovemaking was built on foundations of knowledge, trust and deep, deep understanding. When starting a new relationship it is natural to feel wary as sexual intimacy – when it is not purely casual – is about opening your heart to a new partner as candidly as you reveal your body. Sometimes, two people want different things from a relationship. Some may be looking for long-term commitment while others are only seeking short-term gratification. As long as you are in tune together that's fine. If you want more than your partner is able to give, however, you may find you end up getting hurt. Communication is all important here.

Hobbies that involve joining groups or taking classes are an excellent way of meeting like-minded people with whom there is a good chance you have a lot in common.

Hobbies can help you keep fit (eg gardening, DIY, playing team sports, swimming, golf, bowling, tennis, rambling, jogging, dancing, going to the gym), they can exercise your mind (eg doing crosswords, studying for an exam in a subject that interests you, teaching yourself chess or Egyptian hieroglyphics) and can even provide extra income (eg creative writing, buying and selling antiques or stamps). Hobbies can also be spiritually rewarding (eg voluntary work).

Safer sex

When starting a new sexual relationship – whether it is likely to be a long-term friendship or a casual affair – you need to protect yourself from sexually transmissible infections and, possibly, from unplanned pregnancy.

If it is a number of years since you last embarked on a new relationship, you need to be aware that the situation regarding sexually transmissible diseases may have changed considerably within that time. Newer, more dangerous, diseases (such as HIV and hepatitis B) have come onto the scene. Whatever the publicity surrounding them, these conditions do not affect only young people, gay men or drug users. Everyone is potentially at risk – for in sleeping with a new partner you are also exposing yourself to any infections that any of their former partners may have had. So you should always be careful. Use a condom, or another barrier method, for at least six months and if the relationship looks set to continue, have a full medical check-up before assuming that you are both free from risk.

For older women, it is important to be aware that, even though a woman in her early 50s who is approaching the menopause is less than half as fertile as a woman in her 20s, she might still become pregnant. Although the menopause signals the end of your fertile life, many women continue to produce small surges of oestrogen after their last period has occurred. Although unusual, these surges can still be enough to trigger the occasional release of an egg. If you do not wish to become pregnant, you need to use a reliable method of contraception for at least one year after your last period – as long as this takes you over the age of 50. If you are still under 50, you should use contraception for a total of two years after your last period.

A number of different contraceptive options are available, including the condom, diaphragm, coil, intra-uterine system (Mirena), implants and oral contraceptive pills – which can often be used up until the menopause, as long as you are in good health and are a non-smoker. (Women who are taking the oral contraceptive pill in middle life may not know they have reached the menopause until they stop taking if for a while and discover their periods do not recommence.) A contraceptive patch was also launched recently. There are also two methods of emergency contraception that may be used after you have had unprotected intercourse or a contraceptive accident. These are the post-coital (which means 'after sex') or 'morning-after' pill, and the post-coital fitting of a copper containing intra-uterine contraceptive device (coil). The so-called morning-after pill is more flexible than it sounds. It can be taken up to 72 hours after unprotected sex to help prevent unwanted pregnancy, but is most effective if taken within 12 hours. The first dose is taken as soon as possible after intercourse (and within 72 hours) and the second dose is taken 12 hours later – even if this means you have to set your alarm clock and take them in the middle of the night. The newer version contains higher doses of only one hormone (a progestogen). This version, known as Levonelle, is available on prescription or from a pharmacist.

Not all methods of contraception are likely to suit an older woman, but your practice nurse or doctor can advise on those most likely to suit you. Don't feel embarrassed or ashamed – it is important to be safe. If you prefer not to see your usual doctor for contraceptive advice, you can visit a family planning clinic, or even ask another general practice surgery to take you on just for contraceptive care if that is what you would prefer.

An older male, who may not have had to think about contraception with his previous partner for many years, may suddenly find himself embarking on a sexual relationship with a much younger woman. It is important for any man in this position to ensure he uses a reliable method of contraception unless both partners are happy to become parents.

Whichever method of contraception you choose, you also need to consider protection against sexually transmissible infections. These are becoming frighteningly common and someone with an infection such as chlamydia, genital warts, herpes, gonorrhoea, syphilis, or even something as serious as HIV or hepatitis B may not have obvious symptoms yet can still pass the condition on to you. It is therefore important to help protect yourself by ensuring the male partner wears a condom. Even if the female is using another form of contraception such as the Pill or diaphragm, using a condom as well will provide additional protection against pregnancy, where needed, as well as some protection against sexually transmissible infections. It must be said, though, that condoms are by no means infallible in this respect. When used correctly, condoms have a failure rate of 2–5 per cent per year as a contraceptive method. When used incorrectly, the risk of the condom bursting or coming off increases to give a failure rate of between 11–15 per cent.

Condoms

Condoms have advanced a lot in recent years. As well as being available in the traditional latex rubber, some are now made from polyurethane which has the advantages of being twice as strong as latex, thinner (allowing more sensitivity) and non-allergenic. Use only condoms certified with the British and European standard or European CE mark.

Condoms are available in two standard widths in the UK – 52mm and 49mm. The selection is broadened by the choice of several different contours to provide optimum fit and sensitivity. Many men are unaware that advances in condom technology can improve sensitivity. Shaped condoms, for example, can provide extra comfort, a feeling of roominess, or a snugger fit which many men prefer – once they've tried them – to the traditional straight up-and-down designs. The table overleaf acts as a guide to the different shapes available to choose from.

Condoms are available non-lubricated, lubricated with the spermicide nonoxynol-9, or with a non-spermicidal lubricant (sk-70) for those with allergies. Condoms are best used with a spermicidal cream or gel to provide additional protection. Apart from protecting against any spilled sperm, this provides extra lubrication so the condom is less likely to burst than when used dry. It is important to use only a water-based lubricant. This is because as petroleum jelly (eg Vaseline) and mineral oils such as baby oil weaken latex and may even dissolve it: condom strength may be reduced by up to 95 per cent within 15 minutes.

Straight	Same width up and down	For men who are used to the traditional shape
Flared	Wide head, tapered at tip	For extra comfort; condom feels larger and less restrictive; useful for men who usually find condoms too tight
Contoured: wide head and neck	Anatomically shaped for a better fit; flared over glans and snug below	For improved sensitivity and comfort; helps to prevent slippage; excellent starter condom
Contoured: wide head and smaller neck	Anatomically shaped for better fit over glans. Width at base of penis 49mm for a closer fit	Helps to prevent slippage. A closer and firmer fit for those who require it
Textured	Condoms posses ribs or dots	Designed for increased friction and heightened sensation. Use with water-based lubricant to prevent soreness. Not suitable for oral sex
Ultra-thin	Slightly thinner latex	For greater sensitivity; only for experienced users
Super-strong	Thicker latex (eg 50% thicker than normal)	For extra-vigorous sex (for example between two men)
Non-spermicide lubricant		For use if either partner is allergic to spermicides
With integral applicator		For those who prefer a no-touch technique, who have difficulty applying a normal condom, or who regularly burst condoms on opening the packet or donning the condom
Polyurethane		For improved sensitivity and for those who are allergic to latex

Improving sensitivity

Gel charging can boost sensitivity to give a more natural sensation – almost as if a condom is not being used. Gel charging involves putting a small amount of water-based lubricating gel (around one teaspoon or 5ml) inside the condom before putting it on in the usual way. It helps to warm the tube of gel in warm water first so it isn't too cold. During love-making, the gel warms further and liquefies to provide extra stimulation. Gel charging should only be tried with a shaped condom (contoured or flared) which retain the gel more easily and making slipping less likely during use.

The female condom

The female condom is a pre-lubricated, loose fitting, disposable, polyurethane sheath. It is designed to fit inside the vagina and acts as both a contraceptive and a barrier against sexually transmitted infections. It contains two flexible rings, one of which is attached and remains outside the body, where it lies flat against the vulva during sex. The smaller, inner ring sits loosely inside the sheath and is used to help insertion. It sits up high in the vagina, and holds the sheath in position beyond the pubic bone.

The female condom seems to be as effective as other barrier methods of contraception against both pregnancy and sexually transmissible infections. When used carefully, the failure rate may be as little as two pregnancies per hundred women using them, but can be as high as 15 failures per hundred users over the course of a year. It is important to make sure that the penis enters the female condom, rather than slipping down between it and the vaginal wall. During use, ensure the condom does not get pushed too far into the female – the open end must stay outside the vagina during sex This can be checked by feeling regularly. Some women like to reach down and hold the outside ring themselves during sex.

Each female condom should only be used once and must be changed for each additional act of intercourse in the same session. The chance of a female condom bursting is only around 1 in 1000. It has the advantages of not being dependent on erection for successful use, and can therefore be inserted just before sexual activity starts rather than during it. It helps to protect the vagina from friction abrasions and also helps to protect against sexually transmissible diseases. Although it does not require additional spermicide, adding a spermicide increases the protection it offers. For the male, there is less loss of sensitivity during use than with latex male condoms, and he does not have to withdraw immediately after ejaculation.

Communication

Sex and contraception are embarrassing to talk about, and some people who find it difficult to discuss taking precautions are more likely to avoid the issue altogether. They may even prefer to risk an unwanted pregnancy or sexual infection rather than talk about such an embarrassing topic. And it's not just embarrassment at discussing contraception with a doctor or family planning nurse – many people find it difficult asking a new partner to use a condom in a passionate moment. If you find this embarrassing, make sure you are protected against pregnancy with a reliable method of contraception inserted or taken beforehand. Then, carry a few condoms with you and practice what you are going to say in advance. Suggestions include:

■ Do you have your own condoms? If not I've got one you can use.
■ Here's a condom. Hope you don't mind but we'd better not go any further without one.
■ Before we go any further, we'd better get one of these on you ….

Don't be embarrassed or afraid to bring up the subject – it is your sexual health that is at stake. You are doing your new partner a favour, too.

Masturbation

Many people choose to remain celibate while some may never have met anyone with whom they wished to share sexual feelings. When a partner is not physically or emotionally available, masturbation is important to help you cope with your natural sexual desires. Don't feel guilty about this – it is a normal activity that most adults enjoy on a regular basis – even many who are in an on-going, long-term relationship.

Virtually everyone experiences their first orgasm through masturbation. Masturbation simply means the manipulation and stimulation of sexual organs to produce an orgasm. It is a natural, healthy activity that is important for adults who are not in a regular relationship. It is also frequently enjoyed by couples who consider mutual masturbation to be an important part of their foreplay.

Surveys reveal that 80 per cent of adults males masturbate regularly – 13 per cent more than three times per week, 25 per cent between one and three times per week and 15 per cent between two and three times per month. Men who aren't sexually active and who don't masturbate will eventually experience a wet dream in which excess secretions are ejaculated from the body.

Many people are as unadventurous when masturbating as they are when making love. The activity that is usually carried out speedily and somewhat furtively, rather than explored as an art form in its own right.

Self-pleasuring is an ideal time to experiment with new fantasies, different ways of stimulating your body and learning to delay orgasm to reach an exquisite climax. It is just as important to set the scene and put aside adequate time when making love to yourself as it is when enjoying sex with a partner. Light candles, play relaxing music – or indulge in a warm aromatherapy bath to heighten the sensual experience.

A male usually masturbates by moving one or both hands up and down the shaft of his penis. He may also rub the fold of skin – the frenulum – that attaches the foreskin to the tip of the penis underneath. Instead of concentrating solely on your penis, let your hands stroke your chest, abdomen, thighs, scrotum, perineum, buttocks and even your anus as well. As you become more aroused and approach ejaculation, slow down to prolong these pleasurable feelings. Learn to bring yourself to the edge of orgasm, and then retreat, several times. Also try experimenting with lotions, massage oils and talcum powder to experience different sensations on different parts of your body. You may find it even more arousing to watch yourself by positioning a full-length mirror beside the bed.

For some women, masturbation is the only way they can achieve an orgasm. Whether alone or with a partner, a woman usually masturbates by stimulating her clitoris with a lubricated finger or a vibrator. She may also caress her breasts, nipples, inner thighs and the lips of her vagina to increase arousal. Some women also like to insert a finger or vibrator into the vagina. This is a skill that you can help to teach a woman, with mutual masturbation playing a major role (see bridge manoeuvre, page 40).

Masturbation is also helpful where one partner has physical difficulties in making love (eg after surgery, or as a result of chronic illness) and does not feel able to indulge in penetrative sex or even mutual masturbation. When masturbation is a mutual activity – even if the passive partner just lies there holding their partner's hand and showing their support – it can play an important role in relationships in later life as long as both partners are happy with this.

9   Seeking Help

Many people find it embarrassing to seek help about relationship or sexual problems. The people who provide help – your doctor, practice nurse, pharmacist or sexual counsellor – will not be embarrassed – they help people with embarrassing problems every day and are used to it. It is what they are trained to do and once you have overcome the hurdle of telling someone you have a problem you are a long way along the road to sorting out that problem. You have nothing to be afraid of – and everything to gain – by seeking help.

Discussing sexuality in later life may not seem easier than discussing it in the flush of youth, but in many ways it is easier. You have more experience in dealing with life's ups and downs, and your doctor has more experience in dealing with sexual problems in older people. There are several well defined problems that can occur such as erectile difficulties in males, and vaginal dryness in women, that have defined treatments and even guidelines on their use.

If you have a sex or relationship problem, it is best to seek help from your GP initially. He or she may well be able to sort things out themselves by prescribing hormone replacement therapy, lubricants or drugs such as Viagra, Cialis, Levitra or Uprima (see Chapter 6). If they are unable to help, your GP will know which services are available in your area to which you can be referred such as gynaecologists, urologists with an interest in impotence, or a psychosexual counsellor.

If you feel the sexual problem is linked to your relationship rather than to a health problem, contact Relate, the couples counselling charity.

The local number will be in the telephone directory. Relate has a number of counsellors and sex therapists who are trained to help anyone cope with a relationship or sexual problem – sympathetically and in confidence.

Counselling

Couples with profound sexual problems will benefit from referral to a psychosexual or relationship counsellor. Unlike relatives and friends, a professional therapist will provide a sympathetic listening ear without judgement, prejudice or jumping in with their own thoughts and experiences.

Different types of counselling offer different approaches to the problem. The following overview looks at the types of counselling that can help in different situations.

Standard counselling

Standard counselling is designed to help you overcome a particular problem related, for example, to low sex drive. It aims to let you see things in a new light so you can understand your emotions better. Counsellors will help you explore your options, reach your own solutions and act on them. They don't usually advise you what to do.

Counselling is helpful if you:

- need help overcoming a specific problem such as alcohol abuse or an extremely stressful situation;
- need help untangling the web of emotions surrounding a particular situation;
- are in a crisis;
- feel anxious or depressed.

Psychotherapy

Psychotherapy involves a more in-depth, longer course of treatment than counselling. It is based on the belief that what happened to you as a child (eg your parents' expectations of you, your place in the family pecking order, your emotional interactions with family and school friends) have a major effect on your personality and behaviour patterns in adulthood. Psychotherapy probes your subconscious feelings to explore your memories, dreams, fears, desires and fantasies. Different therapists use different techniques, which may involve free association (reporting everything that comes into your head while you are relaxed, no matter how trivial, unpleasant or embarrassing it may seem), transference (a process in which you 'transfer' your emotions for other people onto the therapist, so you subconsciously reveal your anger, hurt or resentment), interpreting your dreams or hypnotherapy.

Psychotherapy is helpful if you:

- feel stuck in a rut;
- have a long-standing, deep-seated problem;
- would like to feel more confident;
- feel cut off from your emotions;
- want to know yourself better;
- would like to change the way you behave;
- suffer from anxiety, depression, an obsessive compulsive disorder, a phobia, addiction or eating problem.

Person-centred psychotherapy

This therapy helps you to tune in to your own untapped, internal resources so you develop a more positive self-image and reach self-fulfilment. The therapist generates an unconditional, positive warmth towards you, together with an empathy and genuineness that accepts you as you are. Therapy can help you become more spontaneous, less introverted and more in control as a result of feeling understood and valued by the therapist.

Person centred psychotherapy is helpful if you:

- often feel worthless or unloved;
- would value a close, caring friendship where you can talk person-to-person;

- find it difficult to accept compliments;
- feel little satisfaction with your life;
- feel you need space to grow;
- feel you have hidden resources;
- find it difficult to talk about your feelings.

Art psychotherapy

Art psychotherapy helps you explore your feelings and develop a deeper self-awareness by expressing yourself in a non-verbal way. This may take the form of painting, drawing or modelling (art therapy); singing or playing musical instruments (music therapy); dancing (dance movement therapy) or acting (drama therapy). Talent is not important – the therapist analyses how you express yourself to reveal the inner conflicts preventing you from leading a fulfilling life.

Art psychotherapy is helpful if you:

- find it difficult to express how you feel in words alone;
- want to develop a strong sense of yourself without the need for too much conventional talk counselling.

Transactional analysis therapy

Transactional analysis centres around the belief that everyone has three basic personality traits: parent, adult and child. One of these emotional states is to the fore at any one time, and problems arise when you adopt one that is inappropriate for a particular situation. The therapist helps you understand which personality trait is active at any one time so you can understand and change any harmful patterns.

Transactional analysis therapy is helpful if you:

- lead a life that is all work and no play;
- are continually seeking excitement and failing to find satisfaction;
- are excessively clinging;
- are very strict and authoritarian;
- hate or can't cope with responsibility.

Behaviour therapy

Behavioural therapy helps you overcome harmful and negative behaviour patterns. It involves relaxation techniques and developing positive thoughts in place of negative ones. Cognitive therapy is similar to behaviour therapy but delves deeper and explores some of the reasons why a particular problem has arisen. Psychosexual therapy is a form of behaviour therapy in which a couple are counselled about relationship and sexual difficulties. Psychosexual therapy may involve sensate focussing techniques as described below. You may also be encouraged to identify and resolve emotional conflicts – past and present – that may be affecting your sex drive.

Psychosexual therapy is very helpful for treating:

- low sex drive;
- premature or retarded ejaculation;
- some forms of impotence;
- pain and tenseness during sex;
- difficulty reaching orgasm.

Sensate focusing

Psychosexual therapists often suggest a series of sexual exercises – known as sensate focusing, or pleasuring – for a couple to do at home. This is a well tried and tested technique to help couples progress from kissing and cuddling to penetrative sex at their own pace and only when both partners are ready. It involves setting aside time to explore each other's body, stroking, massaging and giving pleasure while communicating what you like and how it makes you feel.

At first, penetrative sex is banned and a couple takes turns to caress and explore each other's body during foreplay. You are encouraged to spend around an hour giving each other pleasure through massage (see page 34), but avoiding obviously erotic areas such as the breasts and genitals. Use all five senses – touch, taste, smell, sight and sound. Tell your partner what you like and how it could be better. After a while, swap places, and touch your partner in the way that gives you pleasure to see how they respond. Once both partners are comfortable with this, you can progress to the next stage, in which erogenous zones can be touched as well.

Mutual masturbation is allowed, but full intercourse remains out of bounds. This takes away any pressure to perform and allows both partners to relax without fear that intercourse has to be attempted. Eventually, sometimes after more than 20 sessions, lasting an hour each, you may feel ready to try penetration – but without movement (ie thrusting). This exercise aims to prove that orgasm is not essential with penetration. After you are both aroused, the female guides the man's penis into her vagina, and is allowed to contract her pelvic floor muscles but nothing else. The man is banned from thrusting. You should remain coupled but still for several minutes, and disengage before orgasm. You can repeat penetration as often as you wish, as long as there is no movement once inside. This helps to prolong the phase of giving one another pleasure. Orgasm may then be reached through mutual masturbation but without penetration. Finally, penetration with movement is allowed. After the penis is inserted into the vagina, only the woman is allowed to move at first. Then she should lie still and the man is allowed to make slow, gentle movements. Continue taking turns before withdrawing every so often and continuing to caress and stroke each other. The object of sensate focusing is not orgasm, but to learn that arousal can be pleasurable itself, although after several sessions, you are allowed to reach climax during penetrative sex with movement.

It is important to make appreciative noises and smile when your partner does something you like, and to take their hand and guide them to areas you like to be touched. You can also show them how quickly, slowly, softly or firmly you like to be touched by placing your own fingers over theirs and literally showing them what to do.

Sensate focusing is surprisingly successful as both partners remain in control at all times within the strict guidelines.

How to find a qualified counsellor

As counselling services are not yet fully regulated, anyone can call them-selves a psychologist, counsellor or psychotherapist. It is important to ensure that the therapist you consult is properly trained and experi-enced, in which case they will usually be a member of a professional body that holds a register of qualified practitioners. Avoid any so-called therapist who offers to act as a sex surrogate, wants to observe sexual activities or suggests you engage in sex exercises in their presence. It is only acceptable for a medically qualified sex therapist to examine you, and this is only usually necessary where an anatomical abnormality is suspected or needs to be ruled out. If a doctor needs to examine you intimately, always ask why, what they are looking for, and whether or not it is strictly necessary. If you would prefer to be examined by a doctor of the same gender as yourself, it is perfectly acceptable to say so. In this case, your doctor should be quite happy to arrange for another doctor to examine you instead.

Useful Addresses

Amarant Trust
80 Lambeth Road
London SE1 7PW
Tel: 020 7401 3855
Website: www.amarantmenopausetrust.org.uk
Provides information on HRT and the menopause.

Aromatherapy Organisations Council
PO Box 19834
London SE25 6WF
Tel/Fax: 020 8251 7912 (10am–2pm)
Website: www.aocuk.net
For a list of qualified practitioners in your area.

Arthritis Care
18 Stephenson Way
London NW1 2HD
Tel: 020 7916 1500
Freephone helpline 0808 800 4050 (Mon–Fri 12–4pm)
Website: www.arthritiscare.org.uk
Provides information and support on all aspects of coping with arthritis.

Breast Cancer Care
Klin House
210 New Kings Road
London SW6 4NZ
Freephone Helpline: 0808 800 6000
(10am–5pm weekdays, 10am–2pm Saturday)
Website: www.breastcancercare.org.uk
Breast cancer information and support, prosthesis advice and counselling.

British Association for Counselling and Psychotherapy (BACP)

1 Regent Place

Rugby

Warwickshire CV21 2PJ

Tel: 0870 4435252

Website: www.bacp.co.uk

Publishes a directory of counsellors in the UK. Send an sae for information.

CancerBACUP

3 Bath Place

Rivington Street

London EC2A 3JR

Tel: 020 7696 9003

Website: www.cancerbacup.org.uk

Provides a range of services, support and publications for patients, relatives and professional workers.

Cruse Bereavement Care

Cruse House

126 Sheen Road

Richmond upon Thames

Surrey TW9 1UR

Tel: 020 8939 9530

Helpline: 0870 167 1677

Website: www.crusebereavementcare.org.uk

For all types of bereavement counselling and a wide range of publications.

Emotional Bliss

214 Bellingdon Road

Chesham

Bucks HP5 2NN

Tel: 0870 041 0022

Email: info@emotionalbliss.com

Website: www.emotionalbliss.co.uk

This company manufactures modern, 'female-friendly' vibrators or 'vibes'. Information is also available via Relate.

Health Development Agency

7th Floor, Holborn Gate
330 High Holborn
London WC1V 7BA
Tel: 020 7430 0850
Website: www.hda-online.org.uk
Provides details of a wide range of leaflets and books promoting good health.

Relate

Herbert Gray College
Little Church Street
Rugby
Warwickshire CV21 3AP
Tel: 01788 73241
Helpline (Relateline) 0845 130 40 10
Website: www.relate.org.uk

Relate – in Scotland

Tel: 0131 558 9669
Website: www.couplecounselling.org

Royal College of Psychiatrists

17 Belgrave Square
London SW1X 8PG
Tel: 020 7235 2351
Website: www.rcpsych.ac.uk
Publishes a range of information for dealing with anxieties, phobias, depression and bereavement.

Samaritans

Tel: 0345 909090
Website: www.samaritans.org.uk

SPOD (Association to Aid the Sexual and Personal Relationships of People with a Disability)

286 Camden Road
London N7 0BJ

Tel: 020 7607 8851

Telephone counselling: Monday and Wednesday 1.30–4.30pm; Tuesday and Thursday 10.30am–1.30pm.

Website: www.spod-uk.org

Advice and information on sexual and personal relationships for people with a disability.

University of the Third Age (U3A)

National Office

19 East Street

Bromley

Kent BR1 1QH

Tel: 020 8466 6139

Fax: 020 8466 5749

Website: www.u3a.org.uk

Day-time study and recreational classes. Send a sae for further information about classes for older people, or look in the telephone directory for local branch.

About Age Concern

Intimate Relations: living and loving in later life is one of a wide range of publications produced by Age Concern England, the National Council on Ageing. Age Concern works on behalf of all older people and believes later life should be fulfilling and enjoyable. For too many this is impossible. As the leading charitable movement in the UK concerned with ageing and older people, Age Concern finds effective ways to change that situation.

Where possible, we enable older people to solve problems themselves, providing as much or as little support as they need. A network of local Age Concerns, supported by many thousands of volunteers, provides community-based services such as lunch clubs, day centres and home visiting.

Nationally, we take a lead role in campaigning, parliamentary work, policy analysis, research, specialist information and advice provision, and publishing. Innovative programmes promote healthier lifestyles and provide older people with opportunities to give the experience of a lifetime back to their communities.

Age Concern is dependent on donations, covenants and legacies.

Age Concern England
1268 London Road
London SW16 4ER
Tel: 020 8765 7200
Fax: 020 8765 7211
Website:
www.ageconcern.org.uk

Age Concern Cymru
4th Floor
1 Cathedral Road
Cardiff CF11 9SD
Fax: 029 2039 9562
Website:www.accymru.org.uk

Age Concern Scotland
113 Rose Street
Edinburgh EH2 3DT
Tel: 0131 220 3345
Fax: 0131 220 2779
Website:
www.ageconcernscotland.org.uk

Age Concern Northern Ireland
3 Lower Crescent
Belfast BT7 1NR
Fax: 028 9023 5497
Website:
www.ageconcernni.org

Publications from Age Concern Books

Better Health in Retirement

Dr Anne Roberts

Retirement can be a time of great activity – and many people wonder how they found time to work. It can also be a time when people face greater health difficulties. It is important, therefore, that we continue to look after our health – or break the bad habits that we have built up over the years – so that we can look forward to a long and healthy retirement. Topics covered include:

- developing a healthy lifestyle
- health checks and screening
- common illnesses in later life
- using the health service
- help for older carers.

£6.99 0-86242-251-5

Know Your Complementary Therapies

Eileen Inge Herzberg

People who practise natural medicine have many different ideas and philosophies, but they all share a common basic belief: that we can all heal ourselves – we just need a little help from time to time.

Written in clear, jargon-free language, the book covers an introduction to complementary therapies, including acupuncture, herbal medicine, aromatherapy, spiritual healing, homeopathy and osteopathy. Uniquely focusing on complementary therapies and older people, the book helps readers to decide which therapies are best suited to their needs, and where to go for help.

£9.99 0-86242-309-0

Gardening in Retirement

Bernard Salt

Gardening in Retirement is a new and refreshing approach to gardening, aimed specifically at retired people. It is a book for the fit and active looking for a challenge, but it also contains information useful for those who experience difficulties with everyday tasks. The book:

■   contains numerous ideas and tips on making most jobs easier

■   covers both organic and conventional approaches to gardening

■   contains over 300 colour photographs.

Subject covers include patios, lawns, borders, greenhouses, trees, fruit and vegetables. Safety recycling, care of wildlife and the environment are also emphasised. Highly practical, the book has something to offer everyone – from those who want to spend happy hours pursuing gardening as a hobby to others who want an easy-to-maintain yet attractive garden.

£9.99 0-86242-311-2

How to be a Silver Surfer: A beginner's guide to the internet

Emma Aldridge

This bestselling guide has been completely revised and updated, with new chapters on shopping, banking, family trees and gardening, all using the Internet. It is a companion guide for people who are new to the Internet and a little apprehensive about what to do. Using simple step-by-step explanations, it will 'hand-hold' readers through the most important tasks when first using the Internet. Topics include searching the web, sending an email and saving a favourite web page for future reference.

Aimed at the over 50s, the emphasis is on using the Internet as a tool to enrich existing interests, such as travel, fishing, aromatherapy, cooking and furniture restoration, and as a recreational activity in itself, including on-line bridge, emailing family and friends, and chat sites. It can also ensure you don't miss out on good deals and last minute bargains.

£5.99 0-86242-379-1

If you would like to order any of these titles, please write to the address below, enclosing a cheque or money order for the appropriate amount (plus £1.99 p&p for one book; for additional books please add 75p per book up to a maximum of £7.50) made payable to Age Concern England. Credit card orders may be made on 0870 44 22 120. Books can also be ordered online at www.ageconcern.org.uk/shop

Age Concern Books
Units 5 and 6 Industrial Estate
Brecon
Powys LD3 8LA

Bulk order discounts

Age Concern Books is pleased to offer a discount on orders totalling 50 or more copies of the same title. For details, please contact Age Concern Books on Tel: 0870 44 22 120.

Customised editions

Age Concern Books is pleased to offer a free 'customisation' service for anyone wishing to purchase 500 or more copies of the title. This gives you the option to have a unique front cover design featuring your organisation's logo and corporate colours, or adding your logo to the current cover design. You can also insert an additional four pages of text for a small additional fee. Existing clients include many of the biggest names in British industry, retailing and finance, the trades unions, educational establishments, the statutory and voluntary sectors, and welfare associations. For full details, please contact Sue Henning, Age Concern Books, Astral House, 1268 London Road, London SW16 4ER. Fax: 020 8765 7211. Email: hennings@ace.org.uk

Visit our Website at www.ageconcern.org.uk/shop

Age Concern Information Line/ Factsheets subscription

Age Concern produces 44 comprehensive factsheets designed to answer many of the questions older people (or those advising them) may have. Topics covered include money and benefits, health, community care, leisure and education, and housing. For up to five free factsheets, telephone 0800 00 99 66 (7am–7pm, seven days a week, every day of the year). Alternatively you may prefer to write to Age Concern, FREEPOST (SWB 30375), ASHBURTON, Devon TQ13 7ZZ.

For professionals working with older people, the factsheets are available on an annual subscription service, which includes updates throughout the year. For further details and costs of the subscription, please write to Age Concern England at the above Freepost address.

We hope that this publication has been useful to you. If so, we would very much like to hear from you. Alternatively, if you feel that we could add or change anything, then please write and tell us, using the following Freepost address: Age Concern, FREEPOST CN1 794, London SW16 4BR

Index